Mothering Many

Sanity-Saving Strategies from Moms of Four or More

Compiled and Edited by Marie K. MacPherson

MANKATO, MINNESOTA
INTO YOUR HANDS LLC
2016

Into Your Hands LLC
Mankato, Minnesota
www.intoyourhandsllc.com

ISBN–10: 0–9857543–4–6

ISBN–13: 978–0–9857543–4–1

Library of Congress Subject Headings
Mother and Child—Anecdotes
Motherhood—Anecdotes
Mothers—Anecdotes
Parenting

First printing, February 2016.

25 moms of 160+ children navigate 56 challenges that mothers frequently face: menu-planning, laundry, time-management, self-care, homeschooling, intimacy, home-devotions, and much more!

Mothering Many:

Sanity-Saving Strategies from Moms of Four or More

"*Mothering Many* isn't a narrow how-to guide, but a broad how-do compilation. How do moms of 4+ kids do it? A huge range of relevant questions has been asked and answered in this helpful resource. The book provides ideas and encouragement for caring moms who are grateful for more of those things. Thank you, Mrs. MacPherson!"

Rosie Adle, blessed wife, mom, deaconess,
and co-author of *LadyLike*

"I wish I could have read this book years ago! Reading *Mothering Many* has given me new insight into my vocations as a mom and a wife. I appreciate the diverse approaches to mothering. While there is no one right way, through the insights given in this book I have found some "better" ways of approaching motherhood. The focus on grace is evident and much needed in our (and every) day and age."

Anna Gullixson, mother to four blessings and pastor's wife

"If you want a wealth of knowledge, advice, and encouragement from saint-and-sinner mothers, this is it. I wish I would have had *Mothering Many* on my reference shelf years ago, but I am so grateful to Marie for conducting her project and for sharing it now. Many moms—of 2 or 10—will benefit from its breadth and depth of insight into surviving and cherishing this hard, wonderful vocation."

Emily S. Olson, pastor's wife, mom of five,
and freelance writer/columnist

Contents

Dedication 8

Introduction 9

Chapter 1: Domestic Tranquility

Kitchen Tools 12

Menu Planning 15

Snacking 19

Table Clean-Up 21

Dishes 24

Chores 25

Laundry 28

Diapers 30

Shopping 32

Shopping with "Helpers" 34

Chapter 2: Money Matters

Money-Saving Shopping Tips 36

Buying in Bulk 38

Supply and Demand 39

Gifts 42

Haircuts 45

Family Portraits 46

Allowance 47

Entertainment 50

Cost of College 52

Chapter 3: Generally "Kid"ding Around

Baby Books 54

Picking Up Toys 56

Appointments 57

Clothing 59

Being Presentable 62

Leaving the House 64

Bathroom Time 66

Rooms and Sleep 68

Baby versus Big Kids 71

Alone Time 74

Socializing 77

Responsible Older Children 79

Environment 80

Chapter 4: When You *Really* Need a Break

Self-Care 82

Beauty Routines 84

Exercise 86

Friends 89

Hobbies 92

Vacations 95

Chapter 5: Learning Time

Choosing a Style of School 98

Balancing Home and Homeschool 102

Differentiating Between Home and Homeschool 104

Schedules 106

Extra-Curriculars 107

Advice 110

Chapter 6: The "Wife" Part of Being a Mother

Welcome Home, Dad! 113
Alone Time with Hubby 115
Dates 117
Get-Aways 119
Coping without Dad 121
Exhaustion 123
Looking Back 126

Chapter 7: Spiritual Wisdom

Time for Devotions 130
Types of Devotions 132
Children's Involvement 134
Handling Church 136
Prayer 139
Wonderful Big Families 141

Appendices

Appendix 1: Wisdom of Mature Moms 143
Appendix 2: Editor's Answers, 2010 155
Appendix 3: Editor's Answers, 2016 178
Appendix 4: Personality Quiz 208
Appendix 5: Discussion Questions 210
Appendix 6: Recommended Resources 214

Acknowledgements 222
About the Author 224
Ordering Information 224
Mothering Many Facebook Group 224

Dedication

"Behold, children are a heritage from the Lord,
The fruit of the womb is a reward.
Like arrows in the hand of a warrior,
So are the children of one's youth.
Happy is the man who has his quiver full of them."
Psalm 127:3–4

For my children:

♥ GRACE
"For it is by **grace** you have been saved, through faith—and this not from yourselves, it is the gift of God." (Ephesians 2:8)

♥ ROSE
"We believe that Jesus died and **rose** again and so we believe that God will bring with Jesus those who have fallen asleep in Him." (1 Thessalonians 4:14)

♥ PRICE
"You are not your own; you were bought at a **price**. Therefore honor God with your body." (1 Corinthians 6:20)

♥ NEWMAN
"Put on the **new man** which was created according to God, in true righteousness and holiness." (Ephesians 4:24)

♥ JOY
"Let all those rejoice who put their trust in You; let them ever shout for **joy** because You defend them." (Psalm 5:11)

... and in memory of my child:

♥ SELAH
"Blessed are those who dwell in Your house; They will still be praising You. **Selah** (Psalm 84:4)

Introduction

"He tends his flock like a shepherd:
He gathers the lambs in his arms
and carries them close to his heart;
he gently leads those that have young."
Isaiah 40:11

Magazine racks are full of articles convincing working mothers that life is all about balance: balancing a career, family, and housekeeping tasks. Every month, there are new articles telling these women how they can "have it all"! In the mainstream media, however, another group of women is often overlooked: full-time, professional, stay-at-home moms. And among this subset, an even smaller group exists: mothers with more than three children. Sure, stay-at-home moms can easily meet other full-time moms at the park, or at church, or at music lessons, and exchange tips and advice, but rarely (in our generation) do they bump into mothers with more than three children. But these mothers do exist. And they are the ones who should write the magazine articles about balance!

Back in 2008, as a mother of two (before I even knew what Facebook was!), I found myself unsure of how to deal with all of the food-scraps, clothing-stains, crayon-drawings, and other wonderful and bizarre happenings as our house's homemaker. Among the first of my friends to marry and have children, I initially felt that I didn't have anyone to turn to for encouragement as our family expanded past the national average of 1.8 children. I wondered how I could start arranging schedules, chores, shopping, and furniture now, in order that we could more easily welcome future children. So, I began to ask around. Before long, I had a list of about 25 women who were currently raising four or more children.

I would have loved to be a "fly on the wall" in these women's homes: to observe their discipline techniques, homeschool organization, devotional schedule. But with two children of my own to tend, this was next to impossible. So, I did the next best thing. I wrote up a list of about 65 questions for these mothers to answer, questions that I wanted answered for my own sanity and encouragement. The responses were amazing, so much so that I knew they needed to be shared with other mothers. Having and rearing children is so integral to the respondents' lives; they provide the needed inspiration on how to do it well, even though some of them are looking for answers themselves. Living in a society where having three or more children is well above the expectation of most, mothers with many children will be motivated by their answers, and quickly identify role-models among these women.

Mothering Many is written by mothers for mothers. It is geared toward full-time Christian homemakers, primarily those who are homeschooling. However, it is useful for any parent with any number of children hoping to add some order to their home. The respondents write about what works and what doesn't for their large families. Hopefully, it will spark some ideas for you!

God bless your parenting journey.

Note

The mothers who contributed to this book have shared some very personal information. Because of this, these mothers and I have decided it would be in the best interest of their families to use a pseudonym. However, the names listed after the answers are consistent to a particular mother's answers.

With a few exceptions.

There are a few answers for which I somehow lost the original author. But, since they were such good answers, I wanted to keep them in the manuscript anyway. I named these "no-names" Kimi. (This sounds so romantic, with an Algonquin etymology, but really it's just a funny way for me to cover up my mistakes. If you look up its meaning, you might laugh.) The other mistake I made is that, somehow, Lissa is actually two different contributing moms merged together. I'm not sure how it happened, but now that it has, I don't know how to fix it!

The mothers interviewed are all Christian, but come from a variety of denominations. Each has four or more living children residing in her home. They live mostly in the United States, but a few reside in mission fields abroad. They run the gamut for socio-economic status. Information about number and ages of children is based on answers given in the survey from September of 2008. Most answers have been edited for consistency and clarity, but the answers remain uniquely their own.

Chapter One

Domestic Tranquility

"Who can find a virtuous wife?
For her worth is far above rubies. ...
She is like the merchant ships,
She brings her food from afar.
She also rises while it is yet night,
And provides food for her household,
And a portion for her maidservants. ...
She girds herself with strength,
And strengthens her arms."
Proverbs 31:10,14,15,17

While high-profile careers appear to bring women glory and fulfillment, most full-time mothers can attest to the feeling of success after nourishing a small child with a home-cooked meal, seeing a tummy round and full. Cooking, cleaning, and changing diapers may not be particularly exciting, but they are important elements of a happy home. Christ humbled Himself to wash the disciples' feet on the night before He was crucified; surely it should be a privilege for us to spend our days serving His little lambs. Here, mothers describe how to effectively keep on top of the necessary tasks God has called them to accomplish in the home.

Which kitchen items help you feed your large families efficiently?

♥ The basic items that I find helpful are: 1) a large stock pot—excellent for one dish meals such as soups, stews, and beans with ham, 2) a crock pot or pressure cooker—great for roasts with potatoes and carrots, whole chickens, or bulk chicken, 3) a large skillet or large electric griddle—good for grilled sandwiches and making large batches of pancakes, 4) several 9 x 13 inch casserole dishes—for lasagna, ziti, macaroni and cheese, barbecue chicken, pork chops with tomatoes or herb gravy, chicken and rice, broccoli and rice, rolls, cakes, and brownies.—*Janet*

♥ I have a great set of pots and pans that we bought a couple of years ago. They are high-quality, cook the food efficiently, and are easy to clean. Also, I dish up food at the stove (no "serving dishes" for me) so I can make sure everyone gets their fair share. There's usually some left if anyone's still hungry. It just means an extra trip to the stove, but that doesn't bother me! I also regularly use my Kitchen Aid stand mixer, bought at Walmart eight years ago for about $170. I mix my bread and baked goods with it. We're even thinking of getting a bigger one, so I won't have to make bread twice a week.—*Kate*

♥ I use my cast-iron dutch oven to cook things slowly in the oven. Preparing meals early in the morning is helpful for us, since we seem to get a lot of melt downs before dinner. A large stock pot is essential. I have an 8-quart one and it just wasn't big enough so we added a 12-quart. There are times when I wish for an even bigger one! A quality stool is nice so kids can help. Hiring a waiter would be nice too: by the time I sit down to eat someone is already asking for more!—*Ann*

♥ A full-time cook would be nice, but if that is out of the budget, then a roaster! A regular crock pot isn't big enough but one (or more) of those big roasters is great. You can put your soup in it, or two to three chickens, a turkey, whatever, and it's ready for supper. A roast or ham cooked at about 150 degrees all night long and served for supper the next day is so good! It melts in your mouth!—*Sheri*

♥ I recommend a coffee maker, in the sense that it gets Mom through the day. I also recommend a nice pitcher for serving guests tea or lemonade. And good knives. Don't hesitate to use plastic plates and cups for young children.—*Lissa*

♥ My most used and useful items are an automatic can-opener, spatulas, and Kitchen Aid mixer.—*Shannon*

♥ I wouldn't be caught without my large Cuisinart food processor and my Blendtec blender. Throughout the years, I've used other brands, but both of these brands are excellent quality. They get used at least once a day every single day. The Cuisinart is large enough to easily handle kneading two loaves worth (six cups) of bread dough and within minutes, I have dough rising. The base of the machine is heavy, which keeps it from sliding all over the counter while it's kneading. We use the blender for making smoothies and pancake batter. I *love* that it will turn off automatically if I get distracted momentarily with a little one.—*Karol*

Editor's Note: Sometimes it pays to invest in high-quality appliances, even though they are more expensive. Think of it as an investment that will pay for itself over the years by not needing replacement. Learn from my mistake of purchasing over half a dozen blenders before investing in a Vitamix! Also, be sure to save your receipts from these purchases so you can make good on the company's warranty if anything breaks. Often, they will send a free replacement within a certain time frame.

♥ Most mothers may mention certain appliances, but for me it is just the simple things. I have a lot of basics on hand. We have several sets of measuring spoons and cups, several bigger measuring cups (2 cups and larger), a lot of big bowls for mixing, and a lot of mixing spoons. This way everyone gets to help, and if something gets dropped on the floor, which happens a lot with little ones, you have another one handy. It also means that you don't have to stop and wash anything while preparing the meal. We have a cabinet in the dining room where we store plates, cups, and bowls. This way, the children can help set the table without getting in anyone's way or getting near a hot stove or burner. Also, always give yourself an extra 30 minutes to prepare the meal!—*Lyn*

♥ Crock pot, crock pot, crock pot ... did I mention a crock pot? I couldn't survive without mine! I actually have two, and there are days when three would be nice.—*Harriet*

♥ I keep two sets of silverware in the drawer. Also, an extra freezer is helpful to store food.—*Betty*

♥ I've never felt comfortable, let alone "gifted" in the kitchen. I seldom make bread, never cook breakfast, and only bother with dessert when we have company! I've always had tiny kitchens, so I have no decent space for items I'd like. I used to have a four-slice toaster, but someone melted a plastic toy in it! Someday, I'd like two waffle makers (they don't make "family-sized" ones to my knowledge). My dad gave me an electric griddle. It's wonderful to make eight pancakes or grilled-cheese sandwiches at a time.—*Reba*

♥ A dishwasher, a salad shooter, pots and pans (watch Amazon.com for good deals on pots and pans. I purchased a $200 Calphalon pan for $30!), enough utensils to cook and serve with, good knives, a lot of bakeware, serving dishes, and at least two cutting boards. As your family gets larger, so do your pot, pan, and serving dish needs.—*Dana*

♥ Stereo speakers in the kitchen for calming music!—*Mitzi*

♥ I recommend a grain mill, food processor (chops, grates, blends), blender, glass-top oven, and a coffee grinder (for flax and spices, not coffee).—*Sarah*

Do you plan meal menus ahead of time? How do you know that you'll have enough?

♥ I "plan" according to what meat is on sale during the week. As for how I know I'll have enough—I err on the side of making too much; then we have leftovers for lunches the next day. You could say that I "ration" juice because my husband calls me the Juice Police. I always notice if he takes a second glass! But since we don't do snacks often, the kids are encouraged to eat at least what's on their plate, and have more if they want it.—*Kate*

♥ If I don't have a written meal plan, I usually have a general idea of what I'm going to make before I go shopping. I used to be much more organized in this area, but I had a hard time planning ahead this year. I try to keep certain ingredients on hand in case I forget to plan, like homemade pizza or other staple recipes. I usually check to see how many servings a recipe makes, and then double it. We collect leftovers and then have a potluck day since one recipe rarely makes enough for two whole meals. I don't usually have to ration, but if I do, I try to have something else to supplement the main dish.—*Ann*

♥ Ideally, I like to sit down towards the end of the week to plan meals for the upcoming week. I grab several cookbooks and cruise through them, making my shopping list as I go. We do loads of crock pot meals, as well as one-dish meals. I tend to make more than I need and the extra becomes a second meal for later, or lunch for the next day. I do ration the pricier things, if there's a smaller amount. We don't use huge amounts of meat—a person can fill up on the pasta, potatoes, bread, or veggies.—*Karina*

♥ Not specifically. I enjoy panicking about supper every morning too much. I ration milk, more expensive items, like berries or bacon, and anything that will run out if hit too hard during the week since we live quite a distance from the store.—*Betsy*

♥ I plan ahead sometimes but almost never end up following the menu. We have been going to town several times a week, getting two or three days' worth of food. It's not very cost-effective with the price of gas, but it is keeping us alive. I am pregnant with number 12 and not feeling well.—*Sheri*

♥ I plan every morning what we'll have that evening. Since I stock pile in bulk and when things go on deep discount, there is always something I can make.—*Lissa*

♥ Planning ahead is a must! I plan two weeks' worth of meals, but shop weekly for the freshest produce. My kids aren't huge eaters (yet) so we generally have leftovers. But yes, we ration into decent portion sizes.—*Shannon*

♥ Yes, I plan ahead. I've found some great forms from Cindy Rushton (*1) and Donna Young (*2) that I'm implementing. I'm starting to do some freezer meals, so I don't have as much preparation to do every day during the week. As far as having enough, I guess you just figure it out as you go. No, we don't ration; you just have to eat your veggies first! I have planned breakfast, lunch, and dinner menus for years now, especially after having two children. Not only is it a blessing to the budget, but grocery shopping and keeping a stocked pantry is a time saver. Beginning with this school year, I have gone to a month at a glance menu plan.—*Dana*

♥ Yes! Here's a sample. For Breakfast: Sundays—homemade pancakes made in bulk (freezing the remaining for use during the week); Mondays—ham and jam croissants and tator tots; Tuesdays—frozen pancakes and fruit; Wednesdays—scrambled egg and sausage bagels; Thursdays—homemade muffins and yogurt; Fridays—frozen pancakes or frozen waffles and fruit; Saturdays—eggs, cinnamon rolls, and sausage or bacon. For Lunch: We always eat leftovers first, and if there are not enough, then we have sandwiches, pasta, or chicken tenders or fish fillets, fruit or veggie sticks, and chips or bread. For Snack: Mondays—co-op or activity snack; Tuesdays—cheese stick or a couple of graham crackers; Wednesdays—apple or yogurt; Thursdays—popcorn or cup of dry cereal; Fridays—cup of cheese crackers or animal crackers; Saturdays—spoon of peanut butter or cup of pretzels. This allows them a choice, as not all of my children have the same preferences. Dinner: Mondays—crock pot meal; Tuesdays—meat and potatoes; Wednesdays—soup or dry beans with ham and bread; Thursdays—Italian Night; Fridays—Mexican or Asian Night; Saturdays—a meal worthy of guests; Sundays—I leave these blank to allow for some flexibility with church and fellowship time. Sometimes we may go out for lunch or dinner, or sometimes we may get together with other families. If we are home, my family has their favorites that I will prepare, like homemade tortillas or something on the grill.—*Janet*

♥ I plan two weeks' worth of meals before I hit the grocery store. I make my list from my menus. I don't plan specific meals for specific days, but I know which meals I have to choose from.—*Amy*

♥ I do plan menus ahead of time. When I don't, I regret it. Knowing just how much to prepare takes practice. There have been times when what I've cooked isn't enough, so we eat more bread with it, or add macaroni or rice as a side dish. Our family is currently in a location where meat is expensive, so I'm learning to cook meals with beans, lentils, and more vegetables.—*Christy*

♥ I don't plan ahead because it's not my style. I double or triple most recipes, and I keep in mind the needed foods when shopping. We make sure to have veggies (or fruit when it is in season and affordable), and bread on the table as "fillers." We only ration when food is really tight or the meal is a favorite and goes too fast. —*Sharon*

♥ Yes, definitely! I plan a week at a time. I create my meal plan using the computer. I first start with what's left in the fridge and pantry and use it up. Then, I plan the meals that I need to go shopping for. Usually, if I use up what we have first, then I don't need to get much at the store, saving us money. I am starting to make meals a month ahead and freeze them, which takes more planning, but it may be worth it financially.—*Tina*

♥ Planning the meals ahead of time works great for most people, but not for me because I have a lot of health problems. I never know how I am going to feel physically from one day to the next. If I am having an "off" day, then something quick and easy gets made. As for rationing, I don't think there is any way to know for sure if you'll have enough. I just guess. If it isn't enough, then I make notes on my recipe cards about what changes I need to make for next time.—*Lyn*

♥ I should. It would be so much more helpful! I have a few standards that I fall back on when I don't plan meals. How do I know that we'll have enough? I usually double or triple the recipe. Do I ration? Sometimes, like when I have made turkey patties and there is a set amount. I start everyone off with a certain amount and then if there are more, we go from there. Other times I don't have to ration because I know I will have more than enough. If I am trying to double a meal for another day, I have learned that I need to take that next meal's portion out before we start eating!—*Harriet*

♥ We plan dinner meals a month at a time. I can always rearrange things as needed from day to day. I keep breakfast staples on hand: eggs, bread, sausage, grits, oats, fresh fruit. At lunch, we typically eat leftovers and have simple meals that don't require much preparation.—*Laurie*

♥ In the past, I planned menus. I even did the "once a month cooking" a couple of times. With church two or three times a week, I just barely manage to keep us from starving as we run to services! Quick things with hamburger are the staples around here. In winter "vats" of soup that can be quickly heated are eaten for several meals. I often cook extra, so there will be "planned leftovers," at least for Daddy's lunch. Appetites grow gradually, and since kids usually comes one at a time, I've just gradually increased amounts—nothing scientific or organized. I usually prefer that the kids eat as much as they want at mealtime, so I don't have to deal with snacks. I hate to deal with food prep and dishes all day! If they snack, they don't eat decent meals! And snacks are expensive.—*Reba*

> **Editor's Note:** And thank you, Reba, for that perfect transition to our next question!

Do your children snack on what they want when they want to, or do you have specific times and foods?

♥ No, they don't snack on what they want to when they want to, or I'd be out of food! We usually don't snack at all, but if breakfast was less filling in the morning, I'll offer something (usually, fruit or yogurt) around 10 a.m. If they're extremely active in the afternoon and need something, I'll do the same. But usually, I aim for a good protein serving at breakfast and lunch to tide them over until the next meal.—*Kate*

♥ We didn't use to have a snack everyday, but child number 4 is very cranky after nap unless he eats as soon as he wakes up. So, we've been doing an afternoon snack, usually a cheese stick or granola bar or a fruit/veggie. Sometimes, we have a morning snack, too. If I am cooking, they beg for the veggies I'm chopping. Sometimes, I will just leave a bag of baby carrots or a plate of cabbage or apple slices on the table and let them eat as they please.—*Ann*

♥ Not much snacking happens here, but we do have a rather erratic schedule some days, where meals aren't necessarily "on time." At that point, I do allow some munching. We try to eat with Dad in the evenings, but because he has his own business, his hours aren't always predictable. I don't want food to become a huge issue, so I don't make a big deal about it for the most part. They're not allowed to be picky, though. All have to have a bit of something that's there. (Of course, the older kids can eat what they choose, but they normally choose well because they were trained young.)—*Karina*

♥ No snacking or we'd be out of food! Snacking is a no-no. They eat well at meals and eat everything set before them, and then some. —*Lissa*

♥ Unfortunately, my kids snack way too often (which is why they're not huge dinner eaters). They seem to be hungry every two hours. They have to choose healthy snacks as much as possible: fruit, yogurt, low-sugar granola bars, pretzels, etc. Nutritionists say it's healthier to eat small meals more often, rather than three large meals. So, I try to balance between letting them eat when they're hungry and eating at scheduled meal times. —*Shannon*

♥ They're definitely not allowed to snack when they want. That would make me crazy—I'd run out of what I need and wouldn't even know it! And it would be too expensive. But, some of the menu-plan forms I mentioned above include a plan for snacks. I want to start doing this with cheap snacks like popcorn, fruit, veggies, and sometimes a treat from the store that was on sale. If I'm hungry or more than one child has said they're hungry, then it should be snack time. Otherwise, they can drink some water or eat carrots. —*Dana*

♥ We tend to let little ones snack as needed, provided it isn't close to a mealtime. The others get one snack between lunch and dinner and one at bed time. They do have to be relatively healthy snacks. —*Sharon*

♥ We have a philosophy of eating when we are hungry rather than when the clock dictates. However, the drawback is that the dishes are never done until the children are all in bed for night. I limit things like juice and yogurt, and only fruit and/or veggies are allowed after 7 p.m. —*Karol*

♥ We try to follow our meal plan. Snack is about 4 p.m. and it's listed on the meal plan. But, I am also flexible because I want my children to learn self-control, but also to have healthy eating habits and to listen to their stomachs when they are hungry. I can't tell them when they are hungry, but, we can establish a sensible daily routine which will encourage their bodies to have hunger at the same time each day. But, some days they have gymnastics class at 2 p.m. and they are all starving by 3 p.m., so I don't make them wait. —*Tina*

♥ When they are hungry, they may have crackers, fruit, cheese, or yogurt between meals. We are very flexible about snacks, but the children must clean their plates at meals. They get whatever amount they ask for, but must finish it. —*Lissa*

♥ My two children that have later bedtimes can get a snack before they go to bed. Their snack is usually whatever we have on hand like chips, crackers, or bananas. I don't like my children having snacks during the day because it makes them not want to eat their meals. But, I don't know if this would work for everyone. My children are homeschooled so they can have their meals at reasonable times.—*Lyn*

♥ We typically stick to three meals a day. Sometimes we have a simple snack, especially when I'm pregnant or nursing. If I do a snack, I usually prepare something first, then offer it. That way they will gladly take what is offered if they are truly hungry.—*Laurie*

♥ Yes, but I do ask that they get permission for food before they partake.—*Diana*

♥ In the past, when I've let them eat whenever they like, I've found this to turn my kitchen into a revolving door. We had a hard time getting things done in our day. So instead, I've learned to have one mid-morning snack, one mid-afternoon snack, and a little drink before bed. I usually feed my children fruit for morning snack and vegetables for afternoon snack.—*Sarah*

How do you clean up effectively after a meal (especially if you have one or more children in high chairs or booster seats)?

♥ Everyone who is big enough carries their own dirty dishes to the kitchen counter. I take care of the few remaining items on the table. That's another plus to not having serving dishes on the table! Also, I use a tablecloth that I switch every couple of days. It gets a little crummy, but then I don't have to wash off the table and it still looks nice.—*Kate*

♥ Everyone helps out with setting up for dinner and clean up. For moms with young children, I would suggest "story time with Daddy" while Mom cleans up, or Mom and Dad could clean the kitchen together while children are still in their seats. I also am a big proponent of the "clean as you go" philosophy: wipe up messes as you cook, wash items as you finish using them while cooking. Keep it simple when possible—reuse items if you can during food preparation.—*Janet*

♥ A dog really helps get most of the crumbs off the floor and out of the booster seats! We got rid of our high chair after our second child. The high chairs take up too much room; the booster could be right up to the table with us. I try to have everyone clear their own spot when they are excused, but apparently I haven't been consistent enough because they don't do it automatically yet! If I am paying attention, I will have someone wipe off the table, but I usually end up doing that. Sometimes it doesn't get done until the next meal. I should probably sweep more often, but I don't like sweeping! My 7-year-old is pretty good at it, though!—*Ann*

♥ We're still working on developing a system for this since our oldest is only 5. Ideally, everyone helps to clear the table and clean the eating area (and clean the younger kids!) while I put away leftovers and wash the dishes, but I think I might be the only one who knows that.—*Betsy*

♥ The children all take turns at clean up and some are better than others. I have just come to realize that things won't look like Better Homes and Gardens.—*Sheri*

♥ The kids do all of the kitchen clean-up. Here's the breakdown: The 8-year-old cleans the high chair, wipes down place mats and the table, and puts away leftovers. The 2-year-old cleans her booster seat. The boys (7, 6 and 3) clean the chairs off. The 16-year-old rinses pots, pans, and dishes and loads dishwasher. She also wipes down counters and stove top. During this time, my husband and I talk together about our day with the 9-month-old.—*Lissa*

♥ This was one of my downfalls when the kids were small. I usually did the bare minimum for kitchen clean-up and always left it for morning. (Bad habit.) Now, the kids are a little older, and there are no highchairs. They take care of their own dishes. I usually tidy up the kitchen while my husband plays with or watches TV with the kids to keep them busy.—*Shannon*

♥ I think we're still working on this one. What's clean to them doesn't always pass my test! I have made a chore chart broken into morning, noon, and evening, so the table is being cleared and washed after dinner, and the kitchen floor is being swept daily.—*Dana*

♥ The dear children do most of the clean-up with Mom, Dad and/or adult sibling overseeing. Once the children are 2 years old, they are responsible to take their own dishes to the kitchen counter. We don't use highchairs because they take up so much space in the house. Babies usually sit on one of our laps during a meal.—*Karol*

♥ We have one child who takes off food and puts it away. Another child clears the table. The 13-year-old cleans the table, chairs, and floor. (The dining room is his chore room). And our 14-year-old washes the dishes. (She has the kitchen as her chore room.)— *Sharon*

♥ Everyone is responsible for clearing their place setting. I have one child in a high chair and one in a booster seat. The baby sits in his high chair while we clean up or an older child will take and entertain him. We just start delegating jobs and everyone helps. We go through seasons where we assign specific jobs, but then I grow tired of that system because it tends to discourage going "the extra mile." But when we all work together and they wait for instructions from us, they do more than is required and we have more fun together. Our family works better with this system and my spontaneous dear husband does, too.—*Tina*

♥ My older children have kitchen duty. I got a Clean 'n' Flip Zone Cleaning for Kids (*3) chart that helps my kids do a thorough job. I still have to come back and inspect for some things, but they are getting better and better. Some days, though, the kitchen just doesn't get done like I want and I have to let it go because other things have taken priority. I usually pair an older child with a younger one to assist.—*Harriet*

♥ I have two daughters that are 13 and 7 and this is their job. The boys take out food scraps (if there are any) and I leave the little ones in their high chairs until I bathe them after dinner.—*Mery*

♥ Most food messes are easier to clean up when you wipe them right away. One exception to this is rice. If there's rice everywhere, I find it's easier to leave it a few hours and then sweep it up. I have a couple shirt-bibs that velcro in the back and they help to minimize mess. If my baby is especially messy, I like to give her a quick wash in the shower rather than spend too much time trying to wipe everything off. This is where I really appreciate my shower wand (*4)!—*Sarah*

Lots of children means lots of dishes. How do they get done?

♥ We use the dishwasher mainly, running it once a day. Paper plates are used for quick breakfast days and lunches. We pick a cup and use it throughout the day to minimize the large number of cups that could accumulate. The children rinse them and keep them on the counter until they need them again.—*Janet*

♥ That's a good question! Sometimes, I'm not sure! I take a pretty relaxed approach, partly because I leave the house for the gym and to run errands on Monday, Wednesday, and Friday at 8 a.m. On a typical day, I have the breakfast dishes done by 10 a.m., load the dishwasher after lunch and dinner, and run the dishwasher in the evening. The dishwasher is unloaded once a day by either my husband or me, at varying times of the day. As long as it gets done, we're good.—*Kate*

♥ Dishwasher! We are on vicarage this year with no dishwasher and I miss mine a lot, especially now that I am washing dishes for six while being grossly pregnant! It is one of my least favorite chores and I confess to letting them pile up sometimes. My kids love to wash the dishes, though! I try to use cups for more than one meal if they only drank water.—*Ann*

♥ We run the dishwasher at least once a day, usually twice. The kids are in charge of rinsing their own dishes and putting away the clean dishes. I'm picky about loading the dishwasher, so I do that. If we have more dishes throughout the day, I'll assign someone to wash them occasionally.—*Shannon*

♥ We've invested in a small under-counter commercial dishwasher, which does each load in 3 minutes. This way all the dishes are getting washed, dried, put away, and everyone's working at it together.—*Karina*

♥ You eat, you clean!—*Mitzi*

♥ One of my children is assigned the chore of kitchen duty. As my others get older, they will rotate through the chore. Occasionally, I help out and do the dishes for that child to give her a break.—*Lyn*

♥ We have an extra adult who lives with us, rent free. She helps with cleaning, dishes, date nights, etc. I highly recommend this idea, if at all possible. Before that, we simply tried to rinse dishes and load the dishwasher after every meal to keep them from stacking up. Even toddlers can unload and sort silverware. And by age 6 or 7, many are able to unload most of the dishwasher, if they are trained well.—*Laurie*

♥ My husband and children are in charge of this, and we do use paper plates and napkins at times.—*Diana*

♥ Often, after supper, I will wash dishes while my husband reads a story to the children. Occasionally, my husband has offered to do supper dishes for me, which is a treat. Our oldest is starting to learn to wash dishes, and as the others get older, they will start taking turns.—*Sarah*

At what ages are children capable of helping around the house? Do you have your children participate in these ways?

♥ A lot sooner than most people think! If you can teach your 2-year-old to fold a wash cloth, he can help with the laundry. A 3-year-old can help rinse or dry dishes while the older ones wash. I try to find a way for them to help at whatever age they are, if they show an interest. My 2-year-old loves to push the clothes into the dryer and close the door and thinks he's doing a great deed. Anyone can dust and it makes them feel like they're helping to have a dust rag. I should have started chores for my older ones when they were younger. But, I have learned from this and other mistakes I have made, which makes them all valuable. You can't learn without making mistakes.—*Ann*

♥ If I need a kid to do a job, I ask the youngest one capable. There's no shortage of work to be done, so the older ones keep busy, too. Even an 18-month-old can put something in the trash.—*Betsy*

♥ If they're old enough to get a toy out, they're old enough to put it away. Everyone chips in. I have a chore chart. It's an outline that would keep my house in top shape if it was done completely. We're still working towards that.—*Karina*

♥ This is something I've been surprised to learn. I started really stressing "picking up after yourself" when my oldest was 5, the next was 3, and we had a baby. Believe it or not, as the "baby" has grown up, she's better at it than her older sisters are, because she's grown up seeing it. Even teaching a toddler to put blocks away is appropriate. I think age 2 is a great time to start teaching the concept of putting previous toys away *before* moving on to something new. 4 years old is a good time to start having them put their clothes away, because they need to be able to carry a stack, open a drawer, sort through piles, and not make a mess of the clothes in the drawer! Since I have natural cleaning products, my 7-year-old has been cleaning the bathroom. I showed her how to do it properly and she takes a lot of pride in that job.—*Kimi*

♥ When I'm working on a big job—like cleaning cupboards—the kids love to help. I find a way to include them. Usually, I end up surprised because they are actually helpful! But mainly, they help by keeping their own things in order. They are responsible for keeping their own room picked up, cleaning their bathroom, and putting their own toys away. If they can keep their own space in decent order, I'm happy to take care of the rest.—*Kate*

♥ All of my children 2-years-old and older have assigned chores in the morning and afternoon everyday. This is a valuable lesson in our family and gives them needed life skills. I tweak our chore charts annually, with special chore charts over the summer. I have gleaned from *Managers of Their Home* by Steve and Terri Maxwell (*5) over the years. It provided me guidance on what children can do and how to be a good steward of time. I have always been a list- and schedule-maker, but their book helped by giving feasible ideas and guidance for large families. Aside from morning and afternoon chores, we do clean sweeps throughout the day, just putting items back in their proper places and tidying up when needed. Establishing good habits and training is essential with large families in maintaining order and joy in the home. The initial time invested in training reaps future blessing.—*Janet*

♥ My 2-year-old brushes teeth, gets dressed, makes his bed, takes out dirty diapers (from the little brother), makes sure all bathrooms have toilet paper, dust-busts bathroom floors, and entertains the baby. My 4-year-old does all the above, plus sweeps the floor, wipes the table, wipes the bathrooms with basic disinfectant, dusts (but not quite up to par), and empties silverware from the dishwasher. My 6-year-old does all the above, plus takes out the garbage from all inside cans, vacuums downstairs, cleans the bathroom even better, vacuums all carpets, empties the entire dishwasher, sorts and starts laundry. My 8- and

10-year-olds make simple meals and do laundry from start to finish (excluding ironing). I have pretty much worked myself out of a job! I read somewhere that until age 6 children make more work in the house, but after that they should at least carry their own weight and be contributing positively by age 10.—*Amy*

♥ 1-year-olds can put away their own toys and put dirty clothes in hamper; 2-year-olds can put dishes away, clean up after themselves, and make their beds; 3-year-olds can feed pets, set the table, empty small trashcans into large, and vacuum furniture and stairs with a small hand-held sweeper; 5-year-olds can dry and put away all dishes, sort laundry, unload the dryer, fold and put away laundry, and sweep and vacuum; 7-year-olds can wash dishes or load the dishwasher, learn to use the washing machine, pick up and vacuum an entire room, do dinner prep (clean fresh veggies, shred cheese), and set the table completely (napkins, drinks, condiments); 9-year-olds can help with the baby (change diapers), be in charge of a toddler's morning routine, fix breakfast or lunch, clean the bathroom, and take out the trash; Older kids should be taught to mow the lawn, shovel the snow, take on more responsibility with the younger kids, and be more self-directed with school work.—*Dana*

♥ I'm sure younger kids can do chores well, but I've started mine at about 6 or 7 years. My 7-year-old takes turns wiping the table after meals, sweeping the kitchen floor, and vacuuming our spacious and empty entry way. She can also clear the table. My older children (ages 9 through 12) do those chores as well as mopping, laundry, and window cleaning.—*Christy*

♥ Young children have quite a short attention span, so they work in short spurts. The only way I've found to extend this is if I'm working along side them. If I send them by themselves to do a job, they usually tire quickly or get easily distracted.—*Sarah*

♥ They clean up all their own toys and books. They put away their laundry and sometimes help fold it. My 4-year-old is responsible for taking his sheets off and bringing them down to the washer when he wets the bed. They change their own clothes and bring the dirty ones to the laundry. They all love to push the vacuum around; I figure if they all take a turn, most of the dirt will be picked up. They can do the dishes. My oldest even cooks with supervision.—*Ann*

♥ They all have dusters to "help" on cleaning day. Our 5-year-old feeds and waters the cat and helps with dishes. They can also help with some yard work, like picking up sticks.—*Betsy*

♥ We have a chore list that rotates each day. Each child is assigned a room with specific things to accomplish in that room, such as, "Bathroom—clean sink and counter, mirror, toilet. Change garbage and sweep floor."—*Shannon*

♥ One of the biggest ways they help is that they each do their own laundry. Two of my children do their laundry on Monday and the other two children do their laundry on Tuesday. On Wednesday, the towels get washed and the children take turns each week with washing, drying, and putting them away. Every other week, they wash their sheets and blankets (two on Thursday and two on Friday). I also make sure my children know how to clean every aspect of our home. I want my children to learn how to be able to keep their own home when they are on their own. Besides just the laundry, they do 90% of all house work. I have had some major health problems and they have had to learn to do everything, including cooking.—*Lyn*

♥ We usually work together, but I also hire someone to help me. This is a weak area in my life. They all do what I need when I ask them. My older children appreciate chore rotation because they do not get "stuck" cleaning everything.—*Dana*

♥ Every Saturday, each child is assigned a task like cleaning the bathroom, vacuuming, or washing the kitchen floor. It rotates every week. Sometimes, they help fold the clothes.—*Betty*

How can you keep up with the laundry?

♥ I typically do one load per day. My older children (ages 10 and above) do their own laundry and are responsible to do it on their assigned day.—*Janet*

♥ You don't ever "keep up" with laundry! One of my older girls is generally assigned this job. I try to keep several baskets out at one time, so things get sorted into dark, light, white, and towels. Our problem isn't getting things washed and dried, it's getting them folded and put away. One thing that has worked really well for me is storing the four youngest kids' clothes near our laundry room.

These clothes get put away right there, where an older child or myself can keep on top of it more easily. Ideally, if we ever build another house, I'd have a huge laundry/clothes storage/changing area, complete with showers. No more clothes in the bedrooms. It would make so much sense to have a "dressing area" in your house and would save so much time in moving the clothes around!— *Karina*

♥ *Don't get behind!* I do one or two loads each day and catch up on the weekends. *Always* fold, sort, and put away each load right away or it will back up on top of the dryer or stay in the basket all week.—*Shannon*

♥ They all do their own. The bedrooms are divided with a big guy and a little guy in each room. The big guy does the little guy's laundry.—*Sheri*

♥ Hah! Can you ever?! I do at least two loads everyday. Right now, my 4-year-old wets his bed every night, so I like to get that washed right away. I'm on top of getting things washed, but folding tends to get put off. When all the baskets are full of clean clothes and everyone is complaining about having no clothes, I will work on folding. Sometimes, I have the older children fold for me. If I am extra motivated, I fold right away. I gave up on sorting laundry. I keep out my husband's dress clothes for a separate load, and, of course, the diapers go by themselves, but everything else gets thrown in together!—*Ann*

♥ I can't, but I have learned not to let it bother me. If it piles up and we're running out of undies, then I need to make more of a project out of it! My husband will also put a load in if he needs something washed, but that embarrasses me for some reason. I tell him, "If you need something, just let me know and I'll do it!"—*Kate*

♥ I like to do laundry compared to doing dishes! I got a front-loading washing machine this year. It does larger loads of laundry. I say this because I read that they're not different, but I beg to differ. Laundry just isn't a problem for me.—*Dana*

♥ I've assigned certain days for certain items like kids' clothes, adult clothes, sheets, towels.—*Christy*

♥ I was utterly surprised at the help a front-load washer provided for our family laundry. We got one when we had six children and it helps things run so much more smoothly! I have basically always done one load a day. If laundry piles up, I am more particular about separating, but I don't cater to whites and often avoid purchasing them! I do my bedding weekly, but the children don't seem to care to do it that regularly. I usually wash their pillowcases weekly, but their sheets I do bi-weekly.—*Karol*

♥ Do it twice a week and use a front-load washer. Keep the dryer vent clear of all debris and it will dry a load in 30 minutes. We use Seventh Generation Liquid Free and Clear because it uses only six squirts per load and really gets the stains out! I wash all of the sheets together, all towels together, and sort clothes by color and weight.—*Mitzi*

♥ I have received great help from Fly Lady (*6) in setting up routines and schedules. Back when I was doing more of the household laundry, having it scheduled in my week helped a lot. There are times, like now, when my own laundry is in sore need of some help! I can get it washed and dried, but for the life of me I can't seem to get it folded and put away on a regular basis.—*Harriet*

♥ We try to conserve clothing as much as possible by reusing pajamas and jeans when they are not dirty. Then, we reserve one day a week for most laundry and try to wash, dry, fold, and put away as much as possible on that day. If we can't finish it all, we wrap up the rest of the folding/putting away on the next day. As needed, I do an isolated load or two during the rest of the week (spills, sickness, wet beds, etc).—*Laurie*

♥ I can't! Socks make me crazy! The boys are supposed to do their laundry on Tuesday and the girls on Thursday, but it doesn't always happen!—*Reba*

♥ It's fairly random at this point. I think that as our family grows, I might have to get more organized.—*Sarah*

How do you manage all of the diapers?

♥ I have had three in diapers a couple of times. Most of the time, I use disposable. I used cloth up until child number 10 and decided it was just too much work.—*Sheri*

♥ We've had three in diapers at the same time! Felt like an assembly line! I always used disposable. I think we have our own landfill.—*Shannon*

♥ I've usually had two in diapers. I've gone back and forth between cloth and disposable. I love cloth because they never run out. I wash them with a high-quality product. Some day, my husband wants to set up a drying line outside, but that hasn't happened yet. I use disposables when we go out, and for now quite a bit, because my current baby has such sensitive skin and the disposables keep her drier.—*Karina*

♥ I've had two in disposables three times and have switched to cloth since then. I rinse with a sprayer in the toilet, then put them in a dry pail. I wash in hot water with regular detergent and vinegar on the heavy duty cycle. I line dry whenever possible; they take forever in the dryer. Cloth diapers are a pain and I'm really not convinced they're cost effective considering all the extra laundry. Their greatest virtue in my opinion is that my little dude hardly ever has a blowout in them; with my older three, blowouts were a daily event in disposables while they were exclusively nursing.—*Betsy*

♥ We use cloth diapers. In fact, I make my own pocket diapers. I wash them about every three days, but that might become more frequent. I run a rinse/spin cycle to start, and then run a regular cycle, plus a second rinse cycle with detergent, baking soda and a little bit of vinegar. I keep them in a "dry" pail until washing. I also use cloth wipes and put them in with the diapers. I air dry the diaper covers and dry the rest in the dryer. A diaper sprayer (*7) that attaches to your toilet is wonderful for cleaning off the poop without having to dunk.—*Ann*

♥ I've never had two children in diapers at the same time. My kids generally have been potty-trained by age 2. I use a combination of diapers: cloth once they're about 3 months old; disposable if we're going somewhere and for overnight. For washing cloth, it's easy as long as the baby's fully breastfed (in our case for about 10 months): Put it all in the washer, run a rinse or prewash cycle, and then run a long hot cycle. Separate the Velcro diaper covers, hang those to dry, and throw the rest in the dryer. For babies on solids, I'm fortunate to have a small bathroom next to my laundry room. Using gloves, I rinse the chunks out, rinse the wipes, and throw everything in the washer. Incidentally, cloth diapers save us around $1,000 per year. So worth it!—*Kate*

♥ I'm a wimp—disposable! I had received some hand-me-down cloth diapers, and I honestly couldn't stand how long it took to change a newborn! It wasn't even a laundry problem, just too time-consuming.—*Dana*

♥ When we lived in Central Asia, I had two in diapers and was using cloth because disposables were hard to find. It was exhausting! Sometimes, we didn't have any water to wash them. Or if we did, it wasn't clean. So, whenever we found disposables, we bought them to save my sanity! From then on, I used disposable.—*Christy*

♥ Haha! I have had three in diapers a couple times, including now!!! I started cloth when my third child (in less than three years) was born.—*Sharon*

♥ At one point, we had three in diapers since the 3-year-old would freak out on the toilet; she didn't like her poops flushed! We fluctuate between disposable and cloth. I enjoy the freedom to do what fits with our lifestyle at the time; I don't give in to condemnation about filling the landfill with disposables when family life is stressful. I have also had some great success with elimination communication (*8).—*Karol*

♥ I used to use cloth, but all the washing and rinsing when I was trying to homeschool was too much. I gave up. I wasn't sure we were saving money and it made me sick when I was pregnant.—*Reba*

How often do you go shopping for food? When do you buy non-food necessities?

♥ I do a "main" shopping trip once a week. That's when I get meat, milk, frozen veggies, and baking things. Sometimes I split my shopping because of a sale that's located somewhere else. For other necessities, I frequent a thrift shop every couple of weeks for clothes and household things. We order soap through Melaleuca (*9). I get to Walmart for other products about every 3 weeks, but often we do this as a family trip on Saturdays so we can all spend time together.—*Kimi*

♥ I go once a week for a family of seven, but it's getting to the point where we need another fridge or I need to shop more often. I would prefer to shop every 2 weeks and I think that would work if we had a second fridge. For grown-up clothes, we usually shop online. We get a lot of hand me downs for the kids, so I haven't had to actually shop for them very much. We usually make it a family outing if we need to go clothes shopping. I use cloth diapers and cloth menstrual pads so I don't have to worry about running out of those things.—*Ann*

♥ Groceries are purchased about every other day. Laundry soap is from Sears in the big five gallon bucket. Clothes are hand-me-downs. Soap is homemade. Cleaning products are from Don Aslett (*10) in gallon jugs. Toothbrushes are from eBay. Toothpaste is from our dollar store.—*Sheri*

♥ We shop every one and a half weeks at a wholesale club where we stock up on milk, eggs, and staple items, as well as some toiletries. We shop at Walmart every one and a half weeks for regular grocery items and most toiletries. We shop Aldi once a month for odd items that are cheap there. We hit the bread store every two weeks. Paper towels and toilet paper are bought online about every three months from Staples. Clothing is bought twice a year at the church consignment sale. It is kept in bins for younger siblings and handed down as needed.—*Lissa*

♥ I make a big shopping trip on my husband's day off while he watches the kids. If we need something refilled during the week he picks it up while he's out.—*Betsy*

♥ I am a part of several food co-ops. I get produce every other week. I order meat every two months. I get my milk from a local farmer and pick up once a month. I freeze some to pull out later. I get oats and rice in bulk about once every three months. I order my toiletries and spices at the same time I order meat. I shop at Sam's Club about once a month or once every other month. Canned goods, cereal, and additional produce and diapers, I shop for about every two weeks.—*Harriet*

♥ This is a sticky issue for me. My husband has taken over the shopping, but doesn't know a Roma from a cherry tomato. I would prefer to go once a week, shop sales, and work from there. But now, I make a list which he often forgets and try to deal with whatever he brings home: usually meat, frozen veggies, cereal, and milk. I order all our housecleaning and body supplies online once a month. This saves money because miscellaneous items don't "jump" in the cart!—*Reba*

Who goes shopping with you? Does it work well?

♥ I bring whichever kids are home. During the summer, that means all four. It goes pretty well, especially at stores where they offer kids' carts, but it is very tiring for me. My kids are very well-behaved, but it is a little distracting trying to maneuver through the store. One fun part is that everyone always wants to talk to my kids! The girls get practice at how to be polite to strangers, answer questions clearly, and accept compliments! One store has a free daycare room. There are closed-circuit televisions around the store which I can use to check on the kids. I know all of the ladies that work there, and the girls love to go! They get to play with neat puzzles, make crafts, and see toys that they don't have at home. The best part is that it's free. So, when that particular store has the best sales, I get a more relaxed shopping day and the kids look forward to it.—*Kate*

♥ I take all the kids with me. The younger two ride in the extended cart, the older two walk, and I wear the baby. Occasionally, my husband will come along and we'll have two carts, but it goes a lot more quickly when it's just me. They know that they won't get treats if they beg, so they do get really excited when I purchase something special. Sometimes, I will get to go just by myself (with a baby) while the kids stay with Dad.—*Ann*

♥ I used to go on my own because it was one of my down times, but I've recently started taking along one or two middle children and they have been very helpful with loading the groceries.—*Karina*

♥ I prefer to go shopping alone. I have found that when I bring the kids (or my husband) along, we spend more money!—*Shannon*

♥ No one, if I can get away with it! My husband is disabled so he is home most of the time. He and I will go together, once in a while, for a date.—*Sheri*

♥ To spend time with each of the children alone and since I have an older child who can babysit, I rotate who goes with me on each trip. This works well and allows for one-on-one time with the children.—*Lissa*

♥ No one, usually. I sometimes will take one of my kids with me as a treat to them. Since my oldest is now able to stay home while I shop, I often go during rest time in the afternoons.—*Harriet*

♥ I take all the children with me most of the time. It works. Does it work well? Yes, some days and of course, other days, not as well! Picking a good time to go is essential. We go mid-morning. The children are well-fed and not too tired or in need of naps, yet. If my list is well-organized and I stick to it, the trip goes much more quickly and smoothly! I try to pack a small snack (like a baggie of cereal or suckers) to boost everyone on the second half of the trip. When they begin to get tired of the cart and the store, we pull out the snacks. They help us get to the end without too much drama! This works the best for us, and keeps the shopping out of our evening/weekend times with Dad!—*Laurie*

♥ The children come along with me so they can learn how to shop wisely.—*Betty*

Chapter Two

Money Matters

"She considers a field and buys it;
From her profits she plants a vineyard. ...
She perceives that her merchandise is good,
And her lamp does not go out by night. ...
She makes linen garments and sells them,
And supplies sashes for the merchants."
Proverbs 31:16,18,24

Finances seem to be a common reason that husbands and wives choose to limit their family size. However, in God's Word, He continually reminds us to rely on Him for all of our earthly needs. These mothers of many are shrewd stewards of the gifts God has bestowed on them, making the best of their station, and focusing on heavenly treasures.

What are your money-saving tips for shopping?

♥ 1) Plan meals around whatever meat is on sale. I look at the stores' sale pages that come in the mail, or look online. 2) Stock up on great deals. I got cereal and granola bars for $1.50 a box yesterday, but I had to buy 8. I'm storing the extras in our garage fridge. 3) Purchase whole foods. They're healthier and less expensive, but they take more preparation on my part. 4) Find a good thrift store to frequent every couple of weeks, keeping upcoming seasons and clothing needs in mind. Store too-big clothes in large plastic bins labeled with their sizes. ...

> **Editor's Note:** The next book in this series will be *Photos of Home Organization by Mothers of Many*!

... 5) Recognize anything beyond a basic need as a luxury. Alcohol, fancy cheese, packaged food, cookies, steak, ice cream, and even chewing gum fall under that category. I always ask myself if it is a necessity twice before buying things like that. As far as ice cream goes, if it's under $3, the answer is usually yes! 6) Use a credit card with cash back on grocery purchases. We use the Citi card and get 2% cash back. Every 6 months or so, a check comes in the mail, usually around $50 or $60. 7) I buy food that is marked down for quick sale. Sometimes, it has to be used right away, but sometimes it can be frozen. Early morning shopping is your best chance to get those deals. 8) With a few exceptions, I only buy groceries at the grocery store. I buy diapers and household products Walmart. Those things cost a lot more at the grocery store. 9) The kids aren't allowed to ask for toys or expensive foods. Instead, they can comment, "Look at that Barbie! I sure wish I had one like that!" Otherwise, our shopping trips turn into a long string of, "No, you can't have that." The children have learned how to make creative comments about toys/foods without begging. 10) Get to know the people who work at your store. Just from doing that, I've been able to get free food for our school, a free patio set for the kids, tips on which foods will be on sale at different times of the year, and even free cookies for the kids while we're shopping. It also gives me a chance to talk about our church and school. The "bakery lady" at our nearest grocery store even bought a birthday gift for my son.—*Kate*

♥ Stick to your list with only rare exceptions (especially when you're pregnant)! Buy produce that is in season. I loosely plan vegetable dishes and then see what's on sale when I get to the store. I suppose looking at sale papers is probably helpful, but I never do that. I don't clip coupons because they are usually for prepared food items that we don't buy.—*Ann*

♥ No brand names. No prefabricated items, especially baby food. Stick to Aldi and Walmart. Yes, it is possible to have a healthy diet shopping there. Quinoa is a privilege, not a right. Have a husband who hunts and fishes, and be willing to eat what he brings home. Have a garden and can or freeze things for use all year.—*Betsy*

♥ Never go grocery shopping when you are hungry! Try to have an idea in your mind or a list before you go. Keep an eye out for bargains, but always make sure it truly is a good bargain. —*Sheri*

♥ Buy paper items, such as toilet paper and paper towels, online. You usually get them cheaper and the shipping is free if the total purchase is over a certain amount. Buy in bulk and store it in a freezer! Buy bread at discount bread stores and freeze! Buy only when items are on sale! If it's not on sale, it's not in the cart! (Staple items, such as milk and cheese, would not be included in this.) Check Freecycle (*1) before buying household items. Check online for discounts on everything! —*Lissa*

♥ I used to be greatly concerned in this area, doing bulk buying, always checking fliers and using coupons. I have taken a different perspective now, walking away from an attitude of *lacking,* to more of an attitude of *abundance.* I don't fret over our grocery bill, and the Lord *always* provides. I will still buy what's on sale, but I won't delay a purchase just because it is regular priced. The Lord is my Shepherd; I have all that I need. —*Karol*

♥ I like to "make my own" whenever possible. I make things like onion soup mix, taco seasoning mix, and laundry soap. —*Lyn*

♥ Potty train early! Ha! —*Diana*

Do you buy in bulk?

♥ If I can, I do. It is usually cheaper. I always check unit prices and watch the packaging. The box may look like the same size, but I have frequently found that the amount inside has been reduced. It's deceptive on the company's part, but it seems to becoming more commonplace. Building up a pantry also helps with the food budget. —*Janet*

♥ We do with some things. We travel to a big city occasionally for medical appointments, so we stock up when we're there. I get bread flour, white flour, sugar, maple syrup, fruit, meat, eggs— mostly staples—there. If I had more access to bulk shopping, I would definitely do it more. —*Kate*

♥ We bought half a cow from a local farmer. That lasted 3 years! We are thinking of doing it again, but only getting one-fourth this time. It was really nice to never have to buy beef. I like to buy grains, beans, and dried fruit from bulk bins at the natural food store.—*Ann*

♥ It depends on what you call bulk! We purchase huge bags of whole wheat, rice, the large cheese chunks. We get a cow slaughtered once or twice a year. The guys in our family fish for salmon in the summer, so that provides fish for the year. In the fall, we've sometimes had a deer from one of the boys hunting. So yes, I guess we generally "buy" bulk!—*Karina*

♥ Yes, we've joined a buying club with some local ladies. You must have containers and room to store the food, of course. When my group purchases enough, we can earn a discount!—*Dana*

♥ I keep my eye out for deals, especially certain dry goods, and stock up when I see them on sale. For example, we like to buy whole grain pasta, and when that comes on sale, we buy a huge amount that lasts half a year. We have a bulk barn in our city, and I buy certain nuts and raisins there. We buy a variety of grains (and some legumes and multi-grain mixes) from the farmer there, and mill our own flour. We get bulk honey from bee farmers. We buy raw organic sugar from an uncle who's a farm consultant, and use it sparingly. We buy free range eggs from a farmer (six to ten dozen at a time), and pay less than we would at the store. We buy rice in bulk at an ethnic grocery store.—*Sarah*

How do you manage to keep your family supplied with toiletries like shampoo, toothpaste, deodorant, and toilet paper, on a budget?

♥ I have tried every system under the sun! I recently bought little baskets so each child could have their own personal products to take to the bathroom with them but the little ones have already lost all of their "stuff." Some children are naturally clean and organized, and others just aren't! It doesn't matter what you do, that's just the way it is! The best advice I can give is move to the country so you don't have nosy neighbors looking in on how often the children didn't get their teeth brushed or hair combed!—*Sheri*

♥ I always buy double of everything so we have an extra supply. I try to supervise how much of the products the children use. I don't believe in harsh punishments for childish accidents. I'll admit that it sometimes gets frustrating, but kids are clumsy. They break stuff, they spill stuff, and they lose stuff. I don't go over the top about the little things.—*Shannon*

♥ I think dental floss is our biggest investment. I buy everything for them until they're bringing in some of their own income. Then they have to start supplying their own personal stuff. For Christmas last year, I made up "travel bags" for my 3 up-and-coming "men" (then 15, 13, 12). It contained normal size containers of all the pertinent stuff, which lasted each of them at least four or five months. Then they chose to replenish some of their own things.—*Karina*

♥ Our children are still young enough that we supervise closely. I ask the grandparents for personal items as stocking stuffers to give us a leg up on the year in toothbrushes and shampoo. If I see huge wads of toilet paper in the trash, I do some ineffectual ranting.—*Betsy*

♥ We haven't gotten to the point where they use too much of anything other than the occasional excessive pumping of soap or tearing off too much toilet paper. I try to buy toothbrushes when they are on sale and just have a box full of them. I haven't had to make any rules limiting things, but I'm still mostly in control of how much they use. Only the oldest washes his own hair and no one uses deodorant, yet. We do seem to go through a lot of toothpaste, but we all use the same tube.—*Ann*

♥ I've shown my girls how much of a particular product to use. We had a bottle each of shampoo and body wash in their bathroom, and they both lasted 12 months. I also make sure they don't use too much toothpaste. As for toilet paper, we buy in bulk from Costco, and I remind them every once in a while how much is appropriate for them to use. As far as that goes, though, since they haven't clogged the toilet yet, I'd rather err on the side of using to much and getting "it" all, than using too little!—*Kate*

♥ I am usually right there when the children are brushing hair and teeth, so I monitor most product use and see to it that they are not fooling around. We mostly all do our hygiene at the same time. I have pumps on the shampoo and the girls know only to use half a pump, because we use expensive shampoo for their waist long hair.—*Amy*

♥ We go through things *so* quickly. Especially if the baby dumps the shampoo or the boys flush something!—*Diana*

♥ We order most of our personal supplies through a company online, so I don't have to pick it up. I place the order once a month and keep track of needed items with the use of our dry-erase menu board, just like grocery items. When something runs low, the person who notices or opens the "last one" is supposed to write that item on the board. We try to balance teaching good habits with economy, using enough, but not too much. If a child lost something once, I'd give grace. If it became a habit of carelessness, then I would help them learn the value of things by working of the value of replacing the item. As children get older, I know some families who find ways to let their children earn money and then begin paying for some of their own personal supplies. This obviously encourages them to be frugal in their use—or learn how to afford their own habit of usage.—*Laurie*

♥ I just buy more when we run out. Children 8-years-old on up are required to write down whatever on the list when we run out or are close to running out. They've all experienced the natural consequences of running out and forgetting to put it on the list. For example, my daughter who wears a pull-up at night forgot to put it on the list. I went to the store and didn't buy any. So, she had to wear her brother's for a few nights and they were quite small for her. Also, we ran out of children's shampoo and it wasn't written down, so they had to use mine, which they don't like. They are all pretty good about this and, of course, my husband and I try to do a quick scan for everything before heading to the store. We have cell phones so they can always call us while we are out if they remember something they forgot to write down. In the past, we set many rules about product use, but are moving more towards a "grace-based" parenting style and also "natural consequences." So, if we notice a child is spending too much time in the shower I will require she use a timer and stay within that limit for a while until she can take less time on her own and learn time-management skills. We are preparing them for real life. What happens when I lose something? I have to pay for a new one. So do our children. But, we may help them have opportunities to make money or they may choose to go without. We try to look at each individual situation and, of course, give lots of empathy.—*Tina*

♥ We instruct on using smaller amounts of toilet paper when they are still young. I buy toiletries for the whole family to use. The adults might buy their own shampoos/conditioners occasionally, but they usually use the family ones. I don't like the shower full of lots of different products; it makes it messy. The adult girls with long hair use baking soda/water for scrubbing hair, and rinse with vinegar/water. Cheap! They love how soft it makes their tresses.— *Karol*

> **Editor's Note:** I started using Karol's baking soda/vinegar hair wash over 5 years ago and still use it! It works well and is inexpensive, but for obvious reasons, doesn't work well for children who still drip the wash into their eyes during baths or showers.

♥ We try not to let a child under 5-years-old in the bathroom alone for self-care. We do dilute our hand soap, as we go through it pretty quickly. Those foam dispensers (*2) are good; seems like you're getting a lot. You can reuse the dispenser and the soap has to be diluted, even liquidy, to work right.—*Dana*

How do you keep Christmas and birthdays special, but affordable?

♥ Christmas is simple on our part as parents because grandparents give a lot! We only give them educational items; either a group gift or each child gets something small. On birthdays, we don't do gifts. We have the child choose the dinner they want to have and Daddy makes them chocolate chip Mickey Mouse pancakes for breakfast!—*Lissa*

♥ We make sure they get quality, not quantity. When they were younger, we stuck with practical gifts like crayons or even their favorite box of cereal. They loved that! I've always gone overboard on birthdays and Christmas. Simple things like a McDonald's party, skating, or a family party are still costly, but always fun.— *Shannon*

♥ We let the grandparents buy most of the presents. Our kids are still little enough that they don't know they're being deprived. I'm in an online book/music/movie trading group, and any time I land a good kid item, I save it for the next gift event. Last year, our older two kids both said their favorite Christmas present was the lip balm they got, scooters and dolls from Granddaddy notwithstanding!—*Betsy*

♥ We don't usually buy presents, unless it is something little. They get enough stuff from relatives! I like to make a lot of gifts and we try to get the kids into doing that too. At birthdays, my children get a cake or cupcakes and his or her choice of meal. We also tell the story of the child's birth.—*Ann*

> **Editor's Note:** At Ann's suggestion, we've started telling our children their birth story around the table at their birthday dinner. Year after year, they soak up all of it, though I never tell them the bloody, painful details! Sometimes, a sibling will add in a detail that Daddy and I forgot. For some reason, the other children also like to tell the details of what they ate on the day a younger sibling was born. I suppose once they start having friends over for birthday dinner, they might not want me to tell about pushing them out in the tub of water "right over there." But for now, it's great fun!

♥ A friend advised me once, "Always try to get them something they really want at Christmas." She was right. What the kids want, and what I think they *should* want, are two different things. So, at Christmas, we buy one gift for each child, spending around $25 each. Christmas Eve is special because they open their stockings. They almost have more fun with the stockings than the other gifts! Each year they get a Christmas ornament, socks, hair things, a pack of Kleenex, and other small miscellany.—*Kate*

♥ We have tried for the past two years to have the "three gifts" principle, representing the gifts from the Magi, for each child at Christmas. We have asked extended family to keep gifts to a minimum. Birthdays always include a cake and usually their favorite meal. A tradition we started years ago is that, starting at 5 years of age, my husband takes the birthday child to the beach to watch the sunrise and pray, and then out for breakfast at The Cracker Barrel. We usually have a family party that evening.—*Janet*

♥ Lots of family and lots of traditions make holidays special. We give one big gift to the whole family for Christmas, and then a few really small ones, too. If we have been blessed with a second-hand something, we'll wrap and open that. We were just given practically brand new Bitty Baby Twins. My 2-year-old is getting them for Christmas. My kids would get more excited over an activity like baking homemade Christmas tree ornaments than a huge gift. They have a hard time even thinking of something to ask for.—*Amy*

♥ My husband gets overtime pay pretty regularly, so we buy Christmas gifts from the extra in those paychecks. We are trying to scale back, as we've realized our kids don't appreciate all that they have, because apparently, they have too much! Birthdays are always a big party with the whole family invited, but everything is homemade, and no hired clowns or animals!—*Dana*

♥ We spend only a preset amount on each child. We don't buy for extended family members unless we have extra money. We get little items and focus more on the reason for the event, especially at Christmas. It is especially fun to have over extended family members who live nearby.—*Sharon*

♥ Birthdays: We almost always bake a cheesecake, only invite family, and do minimal/if any decorations. We don't even do gifts. It might sound very boring, but we try to make each child feel special throughout the whole year! Christmas: We don't celebrate Christmas with gift giving either, nor all the decorations. We do celebrate Christ's birth throughout the year, and more importantly His death. He never suggested His disciples celebrate His birth. But even before His death, He set up a remembrance of His death. Interesting!—*Karol*

♥ For birthdays, I bake a cake and decorate it. They get to pick their birthday dinner and I put up balloons and birthday streamers in the kitchen. Sometimes, they invite a few friends. Sometimes grandparents are able to come. We set a limit on how much we spend, with more spent on birthday presents than Christmas presents. I don't want them to be materialistic at Christmas, with it being Jesus' birthday, and they get to play with each other's toys, so they don't need much.—*Betty*

♥ At Christmas, we're totally wiped out running to several services daily throughout Advent and Christmas. We have our "gift" thing stretched through the 12 days of Christmas. We usually can't afford gifts, but grandparents give a few, so we open them every other day or so through 12 days and the Feast of Epiphany.—*Reba*

♥ We like the idea of keeping the number of gifts small and doing more homemade kinds of things. We like to talk about their birth on their birthday and share special encouraging words and prayers. At Christmas, we've kept things as simple as possible, trying to keep the focus on Christ. We've enjoyed doing the advent calendar together and reading Scriptures as a family to meditate on Christ's birth and the prophecies that lead up to it. We're working at making Easter the biggest celebration of the year, since that is the time we celebrate Jesus' death and resurrection, which is the center of our faith. We incorporate the passover into our Easter celebrations as well.—*Sarah*

How can you afford hair cuts for so many children?

♥ I cut everyone's hair including myself and hubby. My oldest daughter wants layered hair, so we got onto YouTube and I learned an easy technique that satisfied her. It saves lots of money and I actually enjoy it. I hope to learn how to do more haircuts over the years.—*Tina*

♥ I cut everybody's hair, including Dad's. After nine years, I'm having fewer heart palpitations over it.—*Betsy*

♥ In the beginning, my husband cut our boys' hair (usually nice clipper cuts) and I trimmed the girls' bangs. Later, my oldest daughter was interested in learning to cut hair, so we invested in a course for her and she purchased some basic equipment. When all her brothers and father need cuts, it's quite an undertaking! As a thank you, I pay for her professional haircuts; she has lovely, long, curly hair.—*Karina*

♥ My sister is a hairdresser and I've learned some tips from her. Now I can cut all my children's hair myself. She found me a pair of professional hair-cutting scissors which make the job so much easier! I'm blessed to have her trim my hair when needed.—*Sarah*

♥ I bought a hair-cutting kit years ago and it's saved us tons of money! I usually keep the boys' hair real short; the girls have varying lengths of long hair which requires only occasional trimming. Any of the adults in the household can buzz the boys' hair. My husband cuts his own, but I help with trimming the nape of the neck and around the ears. We usually try to do the younger

boys around the same time as each other for one quick clean-up. —
Karol

Many moms in smaller families are religious about getting their children's photographs taken professionally. Is this something you do? Are there alternatives?

♥ We had 2 family pictures taken in the past 8 years. We had the children's photos taken in old-fashioned clothes, offered as a fund-raiser for a local group.—*Sheri*

♥ We get them done once a year at Christmas at a place where they can accommodate large groups and there's no sitting fee. We are considering having a photographer take us somewhere else, though, as we've been getting sighs and comments from our children when going to the studio the last two years.—*Lissa*

♥ I let school pictures take over. Ordering smaller packages really helps. It was important to me and I was faithful about having their photos taken.—*Shannon*

♥ We buy the basic Walmart portrait package whenever we have a 6-month-old. If it weren't for family members who expect this kind of thing, we probably wouldn't even bother with that.—*Betsy*

♥ I don't think my fourth child has had professional photos taken. It's not a huge priority for me, or it would probably have happened. My husband does photography as a hobby, so we have a lot of interesting pictures of the kids, although not posed.—*Ann*

♥ I'm not regular with it, but we have professional pictures taken at Christmas. I would rather have great photos of all of us together. However, I have thousands of digital pictures of each of the kids. We are fortunate, because our friend is a photographer and does it for free when we have the family shots taken.—*Kate*

♥ Not since our third child! Instead, we take a lot of digital pictures and transfer them to CD-ROM and try to keep scrapbooks current and on display throughout our home. Good shots are enlarged and framed for that purpose. Those shots hold special memories that can be shared and they are usually more reflective of our children and family than posed or professional shots.—*Janet*

♥ We did this more when we had smaller, younger kids. Now we don't bother much. We take tons of pictures with our digital camera! We also recruit friends who seem to have a natural gift for photography to take family pictures for us.—*Christy*

♥ Jesus brings life. Do whatever brings life to you and your family. We don't do professional photos. Some of our children are great with the digital, and I'd rather look at candids.—*Karol*

♥ I've had each of the kids' pictures taken in the hospital and at one year of age. In school, they get taken every year, which does add up financially. I know of one family who had school pictures taken every other year to save on expenses.—*Betty*

♥ My husband enjoys photography and used to do some as a hobby when he was single. Of course, once we started having children, they became his favorite subject for photography! I think outdoor pictures are so lovely and far better than indoor professional ones. I also agree that the time and expense of doing so many pictures professionally would be too much.—*Sarah*

What are your ideas about whether or not children should receive allowance?

♥ I don't think allowance should be based on doing chores. I think if you're going to give an allowance, then give it. But, do not loan any money for extras. Chores are simply required because you live with your family.—*Shannon*

♥ I think children should have an allowance so they will learn about managing money. I also want them to learn how to tithe. However, I don't think large amounts are appropriate. I'm thinking about starting my 5- and 7-year-olds at around $1.50 a week. Obviously this topic isn't hugely important to me, or I already would have implemented it, but it is something I want to try.—*Kate*

♥ Ours are too young for this, but we do want them to learn the value of a dollar. We have started some introductory work in this area by giving them a little money to spend when we hit garage sales. I also give them the opportunity to sell me the candy they receive from people. And if they don't sell it to me, I just throw it away after they go to bed! Mwa, ha, ha, ha, ha, ha!—*Betsy*

♥ I'm not sure about this one; it's always confused me a little. Kids shouldn't be paid to breathe, and everyone has to chip in to keep things in working order. If you eat here, you work here. On the other hand, who doesn't like getting rewarded for a job well done? We all do! The older kids have small jobs they get paid for outside of home. This summer, I'm paying my 11-year-old daughter to be my gardener. She's in the middle of four boys though, so I feel like she does so many other things automatically, and this is one way I can reward her.—*Karina*

♥ I'm not against allowance, but I don't see the need for it in our family. Plus, we just don't have the finances to do it. I think it's more important to show the children how to work hard for the family. Our children are needed.—*Sheri*

♥ My husband is a financial planner and this is how we handle allowance. We pay each child, once they turn 3 years old, a set allowance on the 15th each month. For instance, our 3-year-old would get $3 a month. Ten percent of the total amount goes for tithe (30 cents). Half of the gross amount ($1.50) automatically goes to his savings account at my husband's work. This savings can be used for education, house down payment, or business start-up costs, as an adult. The rest ($1.20) he has to spend on his own. Because our children have all their needs and wants pretty much met, they usually just have me keep their money in their account. Lately, they've been saving for family vacation treats and extra things that would not be paid for by us, like souvenirs. In the Parable of the Talents, the master gave the servants "talents" which could also be viewed as allowance, since it wasn't payment for a job. It was a "test" to see what they would do with their master's money. The servants spent, buried, or invested that money and each received his reward for his actions. In the same way, we give our children part of our income. My husband instructs them on the hows and whys of using money properly. But in the end they either spend wisely or unwisely and each will eventually receive their "just reward" for their spending actions. As far as working outside the home, we don't really want our children doing that, so that's not an option with our own family's values and vision.—*Lissa*

♥ We don't do allowance. They help because we all live here. Don't get me wrong; the kids don't do all the work while I read a book or visit with friends. We all work together and all play together. They rotate with what they do. They all understand that the more they help, the more time there is for fun.—*Amy*

♥ First, we do a stewardship class with them. Right now, they each get one dollar's worth of dimes on Monday; if I have to do something for them that they can or should do for themselves, they lose a dime. If there's any money left on Sunday, they split it between church and savings.—*Dana*

♥ We don't do allowance. Our philosophy on this has evolved over the years. But, I believe we are definitely settled on it now. Basically, any chores we would do ourselves that benefit the entire family are the responsibility of the entire family to work together (or individually) to get done. Any chores that we would hire someone else to do (like going to a car wash), we could instead hire one of our children to do. This provides an opportunity to teach them and give them an apprentice-type job that they can learn from. We have paid our 10-year-old to mow the lawn because my husband wanted to hire a gardener to do it. She is learning to be efficient and do a good job and hopefully will be able to work for someone else in the same way someday. We have also not paid the agreed amount if the job was not done properly— also a learning experience! It takes time, but it's worth it! We also pay our 13-year-old to babysit for our date night once a week. She has been doing this for 2 years and makes $1 per child per hour. It's a deal for us and a deal for her since she couldn't find a job at 13 that pays that much! She has learned from this experience, but it has required us to keep a close eye on the process to make sure it was done to our standard.—*Tina*

♥ We're still trying to decide about this. We'd love to hear ideas on the subject.—*Laurie*

♥ I tell my children there are things we are rewarded for on earth and some just in heaven.—*Diana*

♥ We will probably put something in place at some point, but aren't doing it yet. We are not opposed to the idea. We think it helps them to appreciate money and learn to use it wisely. It can also be helpful as a motivator, depending on how you set it up.—*Sarah*

What does your family do for cheap entertainment?

♥ We order pizza when there is a $5 special! We also rent Netflix family movies, usually educational. —*Lissa*

> **Editor's Note:** I've seen alternatives to Netflix called FaithFlix, PureFlix, and Faith and Family Films (*3) which feature family and Christian films.

♥ We make excuses. For example, when a kid finishes a piano book, we all go out for ice cream. I also rely on gimmicks. Arrange toast creatively and kids will think it's a treat. We divide and conquer: for example, we want to take the older kids to the symphony, so we bought four tickets. Dad will take one of them on one day, and I'll go another day with the other kid; no babysitter necessary. Plus, bonding-time built in! —*Betsy*

♥ We do eat out weekly, but stick to the lunch menu. We often use coupons or discounts, such as kids eat for free with a paying adult. For fast food, we have a local restaurant with a dollar menu, so we can easily feed our whole family for less than $15 dollars by drinking water bringing the younger children's juice cups from home. —*Janet*

♥ We do reading programs at the library to get free movie tickets, even though not much out there is acceptable. We also do small vacations, like camping. —*Amy*

♥ We buy a box of flavored ice cream and place it in the middle of a picnic table. All of us go-at-it until it's gone! We've bought canoes, paddles, and lifejackets that are a one-time purchase with no more running expenses. Now we spend the summer canoeing. —*Karol*

♥ One easy tip is buying the ingredients for a favorite treat and making it at home, rather than eating out. This allows for the enjoyment of the treat for everyone, but at a fraction of the cost. Some examples are milkshakes, Italian crème sodas, ice cream sundaes, brownie sundaes, and lemonade shake-ups. —*Laurie*

♥ Frozen pizza night! When I make dessert, or if we have ice cream, that's a treat! It's cheaper for us to buy a DVD than go to a movie, so we do that sometimes. —*Reba*

♥ Our favorite treats include our annual camping vacation, discounted movies, overnights at the grandparents' house, and swimming at the public beach. We also have special nights where we all sleep in the living room, watch movies, and eat popcorn. We try to take advantage of many of the free things in life from parks and playgrounds to bonfires in the back yard, or simply getting together with friends.—*Shannon*

♥ We bought a membership to the zoo which has more than paid for itself after two visits!—*Ann*

Editor's Note: If you have generous relatives or friends who like to buy gifts for your family, perhaps you could request a membership for your entire family to a local museum or zoo for the year.

♥ If the weather is nice, we take walks or go to the park in town. We like to entertain other families, too, and I cook with what's on sale. The kids love having company.—*Kate*

♥ We do not go to the movies, but we like to add to our video library when good movies come out. Sometimes we include other families in our movie night, with a time for dessert afterward.—*Janet*

♥ We love to bike ride! We go six miles each way to visit friends. Sometimes, we ride to a forest preserve. The boys and Dad like to go in the woods and shoot air guns. We like to ice skate on ponds. —*Amy*

♥ We go out just for dessert to save the cost of meals.—*Dana*

♥ We can play board games, now that the kids are bigger. We watch our family home videos taken a few years or months back. We buy cheap DVDs and enjoy watching them together.—*Christy*

♥ Parks, walks around the block, going to the store as a family (just imagine the looks and comments we get!), and playing card games are all cheap entertainment for us.—*Sharon*

♥ We love fishing, hiking, camping, reading aloud, renting videos, having a family fondue, going to the beach, beach-combing, and building forts.—*Karol*

Many families cite the high cost of college as a valid reason not to bring any more children into the world. Do have a plan as far as college goes?

♥ If our children decide college is worth their time and/or money, they can spend their time and/or money on it. We're not convinced college is worth anyone's money. Dad was a National Merit Finalist, which was a great way to pay for college, and maybe some of our children will spend the time to earn their way through similarly.—*Betsy*

♥ Even if I only had one child, I do not feel it is *my* responsibility to pay for a child's college education. I am proud to have a child who is going to attend college next year. However, I feel she will take more pride in her work if she has to pay for it. I also don't mind letting her remain at home while in college, to save money on room and board. And with our low income and large family size, she should qualify for more assistance than my youngest children will!—*Laurie*

♥ We just sent our first child to college. Coming from a large family, I think he probably got more financial aid than those from small families. Our kids know we won't be able to provide them with a full college education. They have been saving what they can and will probably take out some loans. My husband came from a family of two kids and I came from a family of three. Our parents didn't provide us with any financial help for higher education. We had part-time jobs while we went to school and it worked out just fine.—*Betty*

♥ Our government seems to want to pay for everything, including college! Either a cheaper state college will be fine with you, or you can trust God to provide enough money for a Christian college. I don't believe all children are meant to go to college. If it is important to the child and to the family, I think the child needs to have a part in the finances. Otherwise, the individual may not work as hard if someone else is footing the bill. I just don't believe it's the parents' full responsibility.—*Dana*

♥ College costs? Now we're planning families based on how much college education we can afford? That means I can't afford to have any kids. That means my husband and I shouldn't have been born.

But wait! My husband and I, and the two kids I've had graduate so far, got scholarships! It all depends on where you go to school, what you choose to study, and how long you take to finish. We can not know any of that prior to conception. Besides, Bill Gates, Rush Limbaugh, Beatrix Potter, and a whole host of others, didn't need a college education, and they are extremely successful. Read "Weapons of Mass Instruction" (*4). Maybe we shouldn't be sending our kids to college anyway.—*Reba*

♥ My response to this is simple: don't send them! If they must go in order to be better prepared for the vocation the Lord has called them to do, let them work their way through without taking out loans. It may take them a little longer, but the education they receive will be cherished more so than something that was handed to them for free.—*Sheri*

Chapter Three

Generally "Kid"ding Around

"She seeks wool and flax,
And willingly works with her hands. ...
She is not afraid of snow for her household,
For all her household is clothed with scarlet. ...
Strength and honor are her clothing;
She shall rejoice in time to come. ...
Her children rise up and call her blessed."
Proverbs 31:13,21,25,28

Though it is easy for the busy mother to think of children as burdens, especially during their first few years of life, the Bible speaks of children as blessings from the Lord. The stage when the family has several young children is the busiest time of life, say these mothers. But, with several strategies and lots of management, young children grow into helpful and contributing young adults. The fruits of this labor of love cannot be underestimated. The world sees a house crowded with needy leeches; the Christian sees a home filled with gifts from above, nurtured into tomorrow's leaders.

Are you able to keep your children's baby books current?
Are there alternatives to the traditional baby book?

♥ I tend to be like Mary in the Bible. She pondered these things in her heart. I don't have time for baby books, but there are special things I keep in my heart.—*Sheri*

♥ I keep online photo albums and file my photos in folders on my computer, according to month and year.—*Lissa*

♥ I started off great with each child's first and second year. The baby books are lacking after that. But, I did write in a daily calendar for each child's first year. I made that a priority.—*Shannon*

♥ I tried baby books, and they're just not my thing. My mom didn't keep a baby book for me, but I'm not an ax murderer. We take lots of pictures and feel fine about it.—*Betsy*

♥ I try to write things down in my calendar intending to enter them in the baby book at a later date.—*Ann*

♥ I take tons of digital photos. Even though they aren't all organized, they're there, waiting to be put together into something creative. The baby books I do have are *way* behind. But, it doesn't bother me. If the children ask me about them some day, I'll apologize that I wasn't able to do a great job, but I'm hoping they will be secure enough in their relationship with me that they won't care! I have an accordion-style folder that I put special pictures, assignments, cards, and report cards in for each of the children. So, each time I clean off the kitchen counter, I purge the stuff that isn't worth keeping, and then file the savable stuff in each child's folder. It might not be the best method, but there's a lot there, a lot more stuff than my parents kept for me! (Hint: throw away the not-so-good art projects and papers at night. Otherwise you'll find yourself trying to explain how *that* ended up in the trash!)—*Kate*

♥ I have tried to keep the first year current for their scrapbook, then add subsequent birthdays to it.—*Janet*

♥ Yikes! I don't have a baby book for any of the kids. I don't even have pictures of every one of each child's birthday. Is that terrible? —*Amy*

♥ I have a journal by my bed for each child, so I can at least write down the happenings; for the baby, I keep a calendar hanging by the changing table to jot things on.—*Dana*

♥ I decided just to do a First Year album for each child. I'm done, for now!—*Christy*

♥ I write in baby books as faithfully as I can remember, and fill in the "forgotten" info to the best of my memory as soon as I think of it. I tend to only be diligent the first few years.—*Sharon*

♥ I no longer keep up with them. I have some notes on milestones for most of them, but we are spending more time these days on raising soldiers for God's Army than collecting paraphernalia that can be burned, stolen, or rust. Much has changed for us in the past few years since both my husband and I had siblings who lost *everything* in their homes by fire and storm. These circumstances force one to put their sights on things that are eternal.—*Karol*

♥ My friend has a shoe box for each child where she puts their special things.—*Harriet*

♥ So far, I have been able to. If I have something to add in, but don't have the book handy, I'll write a little note on my calender, and add it into the baby book later. Another thing I've started is a journal after their baby book is done. I keep these books in my kitchen with my recipe books so they're easy to access anytime. I grab them and write little stories of funny things they say or special moments I want to remember.—*Sarah*

What is your method of getting toys picked up?

♥ We have adopted an idea from the *Above Rubies* (*1) magazine in which they've suggested to do a quick tidying up before Daddy gets home from work. So, before lunch, we tidy up any mess we've made during the morning, and then around 4 p.m., we quickly run around and tidy up toys and other things before Daddy arrives.—*Sarah*

♥ Usually we use the M&M system—Minimum Maintenance! Before dinner, or another specific time when things are getting to look pretty scary, I'll call a 5-minute M&M where everyone has to pick up the mess they see closest to them. Or, I'll assign an area to a certain child. Or, a room may be part of a certain child's chore list. A couple of times a year, I have to buckle down and give a room a thorough organizing overhaul, getting rid of broken toys, and sorting through the various Lego, race cars, and baby toy buckets. —*Karina*

♥ This is a constant issue. I often ask the dear children to clean up a certain area or project before they are allowed to have a treat, use the computer, or have me read to them.—*Karol*

♥ Currently, we use the Managers of Their Chores system, but we've used all kinds of chore systems over the years. However, our basic structure of three times a day for clean up has remained the same. All children have three times a day they have to do chores. They each have their own set of "chore cards" for each of the three times a day. Specifically regarding toys, there are chore cards that entail clean-up for a certain room in the house that the child is responsible for. If there is an unusually large mess from the little ones, I will assign helpers, but otherwise it is a lesson in humility for the older child with the certain room to learn how to clean up after others even when they didn't make the mess. Since we pick up twice a day it helps keep it from getting too messy, as well. Also, I rotate the rooms three times a year. I start this when they are around 6 years of age, depending on the child.—*Tina*

♥ Weeping and gnashing of teeth. This is a major source of sadness for everyone. I've recently introduced a system where I set a timer for 15 minutes, and everyone is supposed to pick up like crazy! Whomever Dad and I determine to have done the best job gets a point. After you earn 5 points, you get to pick our Friday night activity.—*Betsy*

How do you manage various appointments for all of your children? Who goes along with you?

♥ I always try to schedule a couple of kids at the same time. We align dental check-ups so three go at a time. If Grandma can't babysit, then I take them all, but I pack activities to keep them busy in the room. One calendar keeping track of all life events is a must if you want to stay organized with a big family.—*Shannon*

♥ I only take the child or children scheduled for the appointment with me; the rest are watched by our 16-year-old. I make physicals in their birthday months so as not to forget.—*Lissa*

♥ Thankfully, we don't need to make too many appointments very often. We go to the dentist once a year, in two groups, to keep the costs under control. (Orthodontics are another story!) Eye doctors are a *must* by the time each child is 3. We book early and go in groups.—*Karina*

♥ Our pediatrician will only schedule two children per visit, so we have to divide them up. I usually take them, but sometimes Dad does (especially when one is sick and we have to go on short notice). My husband sometimes has a flexible daytime schedule, which helps a lot.—*Betsy*

♥ We don't vaccinate, so that cuts down on some doctors appointments. Otherwise, I try to schedule as many children at a time that I can. I usually bring everyone with me unless, for some reason, my husband is available to stay with the others.—*Ann*

♥ When I arrange regular check-ups with our family naturopath, I get all the kids' visits on the same day. My naturopath is laid-back and relaxed about when we have appointments. If there's something in particular I'm concerned about, we go, but since we don't plan on vaccinating and aren't the type of family to rush in to the doctor any time there's a sniffle, we really don't see her much. She charts the children's growth, has fun with them, and mainly just watches for anything out of the ordinary. As for a dentist, we're waiting until we think appointments are necessary; no problems yet except an injured tooth, and, in that case, my husband took part of a morning off so I could take the 5-year-old in. But, as I said, the kids and I pretty much travel in a pack! It takes planning and good discipline, but I'm really proud of how they behave when we're out.—*Kate*

♥ We go to the dentist every six months and schedule all the children at once. We only go to the doctor for extreme illness. We go to the chiropractor every six weeks for all the kids. We don't do immunizations. All the kids go with me most places, although when I to go an OB appointment, I might leave them with my dear husband.—*Amy*

♥ I have a helper come to my house so that I can take the baby and the child or children to the appointment and leave the others at home. I try to schedule children who get along well together. Also, my husband helps, if needed.—*Diana*

♥ It depends on the appointment. We all go to the dentist together. We take turns and set up the appointments ahead of time to allow for all of us to get cleanings done at the same time. It takes a while, but it's all done at one time. Same thing for pediatric/well visits—we schedule everyone once a year and go and get it done in one day. For eye appointments, more complex dentistry, or more personal visits, we make arrangements as needed. Sometimes I will take some kids, but not all. Other times, we can arrange these on a day off, or a Saturday morning. We will often group appointments onto the same day, especially for myself or my husband. Example: He has a yearly neurologist appointment for an on-going issue. We try to fit in another appointment or two for him that day since he's already off of work. He might also have an eye exam or dental appointment on that same day.—*Laurie*

♥ It's hard. Doctor's appointments have been the hardest to schedule regularly, but to be honest, we don't really need to go that often. We try to be preventative and eat healthfully, stay active, and minimize sweets. We are rarely sick and when we are, we usually don't go to the doctor. Same with the dentist.—*Harriet*

♥ I make appointments as necessary, and schedule as many together as possible! I keep my family records up to date and research needed shots before allowing them, especially for teenage girls. I do not allow my children alone with any doctor.—*Lissa*

♥ Although we have a family doctor, we rarely use him. We believe doctors are for emergencies. We have learned to take care of ourselves through herbs, tinctures, and natural remedies. We invested in great books by Christian herbalist Shonda Parker (*2). Healthy diet and less stress aid in better health. We also don't get together very much with other families and this lessens the exchanges of common illnesses. God is our Great Physician.—*Karol*

How do you outfit all of your children?

♥ We rely on hand-me-downs, and the older ones buy a lot of their own from thrift stores and yard sales. I would say most of our clothes are given to us.—*Sheri*

♥ We never refuse hand-me-downs, ever! Look for rummage sales and consignment shops. Of course, there is always Goodwill.—*Shannon*

♥ They don't need much. They need church clothes. The boys have one set of dress pants, one or two dress shirts, and some casual shirts for prayer and youth meetings. The girls have two or three nice dresses and few casual skirts. The older girls sew their own clothes so they have a little more variety. We don't attend public school, which cuts down immensely on the amount of "good" clothing needed. To organize clothes for the future, I have huge numbered buckets that get stacked in the garage. The numbers correspond with a little box of numbered recipe cards I keep in a box in my pantry. Each card tells me basically what is in that numbered box—small summer, ski stuff, winter, gloves/mittens/hats, etc. Twice a year, I bring the buckets in one at a time, as I do laundry. The clothes from the buckets are clean anyways, so they're just transferred onto each child's put-away pile. As the laundry comes out of the dryer, it is folded and put away into the emptied bucket for the next season. When a bucket is full, I make sure the numbered index card has been updated, and the bucket is moved back to the garage. During this time I also get rid of unworn things by passing them on to another family or tossing them.—*Karina*

Editor's Note: I've found Karina's advice that kids "don't need much" to really be true! I often think my children need dozens of different outfits to make it through the season. In reality, they only really rotate through a handful of favorite outfits anyway. Fewer clothes in the closet means conservation of laundry, too!

♥ In order of importance: hand-me-downs, thrift stores, gifts from grandparents, and clearance off-season items for the next year. We are very blessed to have a grandma who sews our holiday outfits. The biggest challenges are shoes, swim-wear, and pajamas, which are hard to find at thrift stores. Sometimes, it makes sense to spend a little more on better quality items that won't fall apart when multiple children will be using them. I'm still trying to figure out which products and brands I can rely on to last. We've also done some borrowing of clothes, but I'm always a little nervous about it. There is no guarantee that something my kid wears for an entire season will remain wearable. I keep borrowed stuff for emergencies. One exception is church dresses since we only wear them to church and change before eating. We usually don't buy from kids' consignment shops, either. Used clothing tends to have stains resurface after a wash or two. The clothes at these stores are more expensive than you can buy new things at discount stores. But if you're looking for a quality brand name item, you might have some luck there. So I wouldn't write it off completely, but I also don't have time for the intense archeology and cost/benefit analysis this type of store requires. A person might have more luck with baby-gear items there.—*Betsy*

♥ Mostly, we use hand-me-downs. I know quite a few families that pass on very gently used clothes. I take a lot of time to sort through and organize everything we're given. Some of the stuff gets passed on to friends and sisters, but I use most of it. I spent an afternoon last week sorting *all* the girls' shoes we've accumulated in seven years, sizes 0 through youth size 1. It was mostly organized, but needed to be done again, and there were 183 pairs! Very few of them were shoes that we had bought new. Needless to say, I'm getting rid of about 50! And, I found two pairs that fit the girls perfectly for the beginning of the school year. So, I do invest a lot of time and energy into sorting and organizing well, and it's been worth it.—*Kate*

♥ I sew for my girls because we like to wear modest long dresses that are not to be found for love or money. We only buy new socks and underwear.—*Amy*

♥ We buy clothes that are high enough quality that they can be passed down to brothers and sisters.—*Diana*

♥ We find clothes through a variety of ways. Ask friends with older children, especially a family with their youngest ones older than your oldest. Sometimes people are looking for a good place to hand down their clothes to. We utilize local garage sales, thrift stores, clearance racks and such. We've also recently found some massive garage sales. These are great if you can find one in your area. We can shop for an hour or two and find so much in a sale where there are dozens of people selling their items all together.—*Laurie*

♥ The children receive lots of clothes for holidays, so our clothing budget doesn't need to be large. We stress modesty in choices as our older children are buying their own clothes now. We require "wedding attire" for church. If you would dress up to go to a wedding, then we need to show God the same honor and dress nicely for church. All of our children are individual gifts created by

God. I have gone through phases wondering if I should require them to dress a certain way, but my dear husband has always been against it. I am totally happy with who they are and, like me, the way they dress reflects their personality or preference. I think that's important—like a work of art. I'm constantly changing the way we store clothes. We add children, but not square footage on our house. Currently, I store the upcoming clothes on a top shelf in each closet that my husband added. I am able to store three 18-gallon bins up there. I don't store more than one size in each bin. I have bigger sizes that aren't needed yet in the attic, which I go through about twice a year to make sure I don't forget what's there.—*Tina*

♥ We use lots of hand-me-downs, but only if they are in good condition. We don't live like paupers; we are children of the King. I don't have lots of clothes for each child. When we have extra, I pass them on for other families to make use of, and try to refrain from a withholding spirit. God blesses, so we bless. I buy new when the need arises, or I look for an awesome deal. If the next child in line is of the same gender, then I keep good clothes for them, if the style seems appropriate to their liking. Otherwise, I give it away. I refuse to keep clothes stored for years without them being used when other families could benefit. I keep good clothes that aren't used immediately in a plastic tote box. These totes help eliminate mildew, mold, and bugs. And they stack so nicely!— *Karol*

When it is time to leave the house, how do you make sure all of the children are clean?

♥ Their teeth and hair are brushed after breakfast, and their "pre-approved" outfits are laid out by Mommy or an older sibling the night before. We do a general check before we leave. This almost never needs to be corrected. But even so, there are times when the children are unprepared even with a warning to get ready, so they miss whatever blessing was coming and can't participate.—*Lissa*

♥ Line 'em up. Bring out the baby wipes and a hair brush!— *Shannon*

♥ Most kids are all right, but I have one little guy who defines the term "dirty boy." He tries so hard, but alas! So, I just give him a wet wipe (I keep a package in the van) and he does the job as we're driving to wherever we're going.—*Karina*

♥ I try to do this preemptively by making sure they get cleaned up promptly after meals and art projects, but the system is far from perfect.—*Betsy*

♥ Well, they aren't always! I can't tell you how many times we've gotten to church and I realize I didn't even brush my daughter's hair. I don't have to do any thing to the boys' hair, so it's easy to overlook her. At least I wash everyone's face and hands after meals with a washcloth, so they are usually clean in that regard.—*Ann*

♥ The older children clean themselves. I check the others' faces and make sure their hair is combed. The kids bathe every other day, so that pretty much takes care of things.—*Kate*

♥ The buddy system is one way to do that for large families. We encourage one older child to be a "buddy" to a younger sibling, making sure they have clean clothes, brushed hair, and shoes on. —*Janet*

♥ My girls are usually clean and wipe their hands and faces after meals, so this hasn't been an issue for us. I don't know if it would be different with a bunch of boys!—*Sarah*

♥ Now, there's an idea! I've thought I should take a moment to line them up and check them over, like in *Sound of Music.*—*Reba*

♥ Once I get the children dressed to go, they are to stay on the couch watching an educational movie until I am ready to leave. I try not to make them wait to long.—*Mery*

♥ My older girl does the little boys' hair. It has become a fun time. She has different hairstyles they can choose from. I also make sure we have a brush in the car, just in case.—*Diana*

♥ I don't.—*Harriet*

♥ They are required to do "morning jobs" before breakfast which includes dressing and grooming. This ensures that they are always ready for leaving the house if we have gym class or appointments. Each time they eat, they clean up their place and also themselves. Otherwise our walls and sofas would be filthy! We can leave the house in five minutes, if need be.—*Tina*

♥ I just do a quick survey. We usually have baby wipes in tow, so I figure we can always check as we unload, too. I also keep extra hair ties in the diaper bag. I keep some extra clothes in the back of the vehicle in case someone gets dirty or wet while we're out.—*Dana*

How do you get into and out of the house efficiently, especially with coats, shoes, and the diaper bag?

♥ If a child needs something along, he or she had better take it! If the child doesn't take it, he or she will suffer the natural consequences. I do keep the diaper bag packed and ready to go so all we have to add is a fresh bottle of water.—*Sheri*

♥ Preparation! We lay out clothes the night before. Shoes are retrieved by each child and can be put on right before we head out. The same applies for coats and hats. If lunches or bags are needed, they also are prepared, packed, and even taken to the car the night before.—*Lissa*

♥ We allow for extra time. When they were little, I'd make small piles in the living room and help those who needed help. Now that they're older, they have designated hooks and bins for their winter items. (That sounds all perfect—but we still have those frantic mornings when we're searching for a lost mitten or favorite hat.)—*Shannon*

♥ I desperately try to organize the night before, even if it's just making a list of what has to go along with us to wherever we're going. My older girls are great at setting out the clothes for the little girls for the next morning. We still forget stuff, though. We try make the best of it. It's not the end of the world!—*Karina*

♥ My basic strategy is to never leave! When we do have to go somewhere, I just budget at least an extra 10 minutes for using the bathroom and suiting up. I try to buy shoes they can put on themselves at as young of an age as possible.—*Betsy*

> **Editor's Note**: We do not own laced shoes smaller than about size 12. At that size, it seems that children are old enough to learn to tie shoes themselves. I figure I have enough to do to get out of the house without having to squat my big pregnant self down and tie shoes for several children. Invest in Velcro!

♥ I'm not sure if it's ever efficient, but I do have the older ones help zip-up and shoe younger ones. We usually still forget something no matter what!—*Ann*

♥ I'm pretty minimalist; this freedom comes from living in a warm climate. We don't have to worry about lots of heavy coats and hats. Each child is responsible for her backpack, purse, or whatever accessories she's interested in bringing along with her. Each of the children has a shoe basket in the closet where her own shoes go. Sometimes they start to accumulate just inside our entry door, so I have them move them to their shoe baskets.—*Kate*

♥ We keep all our shoes on our shoe rack in the garage. This cuts down on dirt through the house and generally makes it more efficient when we're preparing to leave. A wall peg rack or cubby area for those items at the door may be another means of keeping things in order, if space allows.—*Janet*

♥ The bigger ones are taught to do things for themselves. About five minutes or so before I'm ready to go, I tell them that it's time to get ready and they do what they need to do to be ready. Meanwhile, I get the littlest ones ready. In the winter time, I keep a container by the door with gloves, mittens, and scarves in it, so they're easy to grab on our way out.—*Sarah*

♥ I have a bunch of hooks—we can't handle hangers! My dream would be "lockers" like preschools have.—*Reba*

♥ I start the countdown. We need to leave in fifteen, ten, then down to five minutes. At that time, the girls start loading the little ones in the car in the garage. I run through the house and frantically turn off lights and grab what I need as quickly as I can. Then I give up, and we leave!—*Diana*

♥ Am I supposed to be able to do this efficiently? Seriously, we try to have the older ones help with the younger ones. And we also try to teach the children early on to go and get their own shoes and bring them to a central location. That way we can all get them on as efficiently as possible. In the winter, we usually put socks on in the morning when we get dressed which streamlines the "shoe" process if we need to go out later in the day.—*Laurie*

> **Editor's Note:** Before having children, I *never* would have thought keeping socks on throughout the day would be so very crucial for leaving the house in a timely manner. But, it does. If I have to send my 3-year-old back to his bedroom to grab socks when we're trying to get out the door, I might not see him again for another half-hour. Really. Or if I'm trying to devote attention to the younger children to help them prepare while the baby is still sleeping, but we have to wake the baby up to get socks out of the room, my plan is ruined. And then, I get crabby.

♥ We have a shoe cubby in the entry way; everyone's allowed one pair of shoes in it; we have a basket beside it that holds that season's hats and gloves. Coats go in the entry way closet. There's no room for bags in the entry way. Usually, we just take the diaper bag, but we always have to hunt for that!—*Dana*

♥ We only manage because siblings help one another. Occasionally, something is forgotten, but that's life. Get used to it and don't fret. —*Karol*

How is your bathroom, and bathroom time, organized?

♥ Each child has a buddy for teeth-brushing so that it's done neatly, properly, and in a timely manner. Towels are used at least twice before being washed.—*Lissa*

♥ We are a family of eight with one small bathroom for all of us. Yes, just one bathroom with one toilet, one sink, and one shower. Basically, the rules are *don't* lock the door if you're in the shower and *don't dawdle*! If a younger child needs the bathroom, they go first. There isn't much opportunity for privacy. Sometimes, a couple of kids are brushing their teeth, one is in the shower, and one is going potty.—*Shannon*

♥ In our home, showers are kept to less than 10 minutes. The two oldest girls have sinks and mirrors in their bedrooms, which eliminates much of their bathroom time. The boys just figure it out on their own. Towels? We hang them for reuse. I had an aunt once who installed towel racks in each child's bedroom, one for each child.—*Karina*

♥ For bath time, I start with two children in the tub and then add a third when one is finished. I try to wash their hair right away so I can just take them out if they start acting up or get cold. The oldest takes a shower by himself and I think he could get a world record for fastest shower! (Sometimes, I have to send him back because he still has soap in his hair.) I will use the same towel to dry the little ones off as they get out, unless it gets too wet. I just throw the towel in the washer when we're finished. Every one takes a turn brushing teeth and going potty before going to bed. I'm sure as they get older we will have more towels and it will take longer for every one to get done.—*Ann*

♥ Bathroom time isn't an issue here—I grew up with many siblings and one bathroom. Now, I live in a house with three bathrooms! The kids are still young enough that all they do is use the toilet and brush their teeth. They are responsible for their own towels, though. Since they have trouble hanging them on our existing towel racks, one plan that we have for a home project is to install hooks on the wall that they can use more easily. And hooks take up less space than a towel bar. After they've been used a few times, I wash all the towels at once—around every two weeks probably. Then, all the clean ones go back under the sink. Washcloths are done after one use, though!—*Kate*

♥ We do baths and showers every other night. Some of the kids use my shower. We bathe the 2- and 4-year-old girls at the same time, and then reuse the same water for the baby. Everyone else does it on their own.—*Amy*

♥ The bathroom situation isn't too bad, since we have two, but towels!? Each child his or her own hook uses the towel on it for 2 or 3 days before it gets washed. If each child used one everyday, I would be washing towels all the time.—*Mery*

♥ We have three bathrooms. We try to keep the main one open for everyone, and if you have to do something longer, go to a less-used restroom!—*Diana*

♥ Bathroom time is not a big issue for us yet, since all our children are under 7 years! The adults and our oldest child all use a towel a few times before we put it in the wash. We have created hooks designated for each person to hang their own towel to keep it dry. For the smaller children, I typically just use the same towel to dry off a couple of them (as they still bathe together) and then throw it in the hamper afterward.—*Laurie*

♥ My children are only to be in the bathroom for the necessities. They are to do their hair in their own rooms.—*Lyn*

♥ Kids have a certain color of towel and Mom and Dad have a certain color.—*Tina*

♥ This may sound strange but some of our children don't use towels. They like the wet feeling of getting dressed. I haven't argued because it saves on laundry! The ones who do use towels have their own and they wash it themselves with their own laundry.—*Sheri*

♥ Some do morning showers, some do evening showers. The girls have a mirror in their room. This helps with time management.—*Dana*

What is the rooming situation with all of your children? Does it work well?

♥ There are 4 bedrooms for all of the children. We only have 8 children at home right now. The girls have their own room, but they usually camp out in one of the boys' rooms and the 5-year-old likes Mom and Dad's floor best. The other match-ups are the 16-year-old and 6-year-old; 14-year-old and 8-year-old; 11-year-old and 9-year-old.—*Sheri*

♥ Our three boys (7, 6, 4) all share a room with two sets of bunk beds. Our three girls (16, 8, 2) sleep in a finished attic that was made into their bedroom. The baby sleeps in her own nursery, which is near our bedroom This situation works well.—*Lissa*

♥ The oldest has his own room—a small, fixed-up area in the basement. The three girls share one room with a double bunk bed. The other two children share another room with one bunk bed. It works okay; they actually prefer to all sleep together. When they were little, there was lots of talking and fooling around. It gets better when they're older. All I have to do is threaten to send them to bed ten minutes early the next night. *Always* be sure to follow up on that threat if you dole it out! It's amazing how effective that is. They *hate* going to bed before their siblings.—*Shannon*

♥ The girls sleep upstairs and the boys sleep in the basement. The oldest three have their own rooms, and the others share. The baby has a tiny little nursery room off of our bedroom—a huge blessing for me! I'd make a closet work if I had to! My ideal if I had a chance to build another home? All the girls together, all the boys together, in two huge bedrooms, with alcoves, for a little privacy. What a hoot that would be—and they'd be so accountable to each other! Maybe someday!—*Karina*

♥ We have a boy room, a girl room, and a baby room. I'm watching the triple-decker bunk beds on eBay; we may need one eventually. Once the baby is ready to be out of Mom and Dad's room (read: once Mom is ready for the baby to be out of Mom and Dad's room), they graduate into either the boy room or the girl room. We are all upstairs. I don't like being on different levels.—*Betsy*

♥ We have three boys in a room with one bunk bed and one twin bed. My older daughter is currently by herself until the baby is old enough to have her crib moved out of my room.—*Ann*

♥ All three girls share a room right now. It works well. There were periods of transition each time a girl was "added" to the room. They each have their own dresser and their own drawer for special things that they collect. Before the 2-year-old naps, the others remove anything from the room that they'll need during nap-time. They have the same bedtime, which works because of firm bedtime rules—everyone does what they need to before bed, and then they have to stay there. Of course, there are always those emergencies, "Mom, my teacher said you have to sign my field trip sheet tonight! Did you remember?" But we discourage them from getting out of bed once they're tucked in.—*Kate*

♥ We have two children in each room. At one time, we had three in each. Bunk beds are a way to maximize room space. We try to keep the bedrooms for sleeping and dressing, and do not have a lot of toys in them.—*Janet*

♥ All my children sleep in the same room, except for the baby. It is fantastic! I would rather have the square footage of our house be for living. I keep the bedrooms just for sleeping. No toys. The boys' clothes are kept in the baby's room; the girls' clothes are kept in the big bedroom. As they get older, we transition the boys into a separate room.—*Amy*

♥ When our babies are infants, they sleep right in our bed. We have the bed against a wall then, so that Baby is either between the parents or between Mom and the wall. Then, when Baby is a bit bigger, around six months or so, we attach a side-car bed (*3) and Baby spends most of the night there. At some point, when our children have shown readiness, we've moved them to another room to sleep with their siblings. Right now, our smallest is in the side-car bed, and all three girls are sleeping together in a special bed my husband built. It is just off the ground and fits two crib-sized mattresses side-by-side. We envision that someday we will have a girls' room and a boys' room where they'll all be together. This sleeping situation has worked really well for us.—*Sarah*

♥ We have five boys in one room and two girls in the other. It's not great, but we only have a three-bedroom house.—*Reba*

♥ They all sleep in their own beds. I think it is important for them to have their space, and my husband and I to have ours.—*Mery*

♥ Our two girls have a bunk bed, and the 2-year-old sleeps in a crib in their room. The boys have bunk beds in a separate room. It works well. They have the option to camp out at night, but all prefer to stay in the same room, and more often than not, the same bed. The infant sleeps with us in our room with a co-sleeper. —*Diana*

♥ Our 7- and 3-year-old sleep together in a double bed in their own room. This works very well. Our new babies sleep in our bed initially and then in a small bed or playpen in our room. After about a year, they transition to a bed in their own room, and then eventually into a bigger bed, often with an older sibling helping with the transition!—*Laurie*

♥ My oldest has her own room, although I wish she was sharing with someone and will probably transition her to that soon. Her relationship with her younger sisters is better the more she relates with them. My 8-year-old girl, 5-year-old girl, and 2-year-old girl share a room. My two boys (11 and 6) share a room. This works great!—*Harriet*

♥ We are blessed. Each our children has his or her own room. And yes, this does work out for the best. We have lived in houses before where some of the children have had to share a room. It did not work well. I think giving children their space is good for them.— *Lyn*

♥ My older three girls sleep in their own beds. My 5-year-old son sleeps on the floor in our room. My 3-year-old daughter sleeps in a crib with one side off, and my baby sleeps in between my dear husband and me. We have three children in our room! We love having a family bed and have always done it that way. I nurse all my babies for about two years, unless I get pregnant before then. Usually around 3 to 5 years, the child starts sleeping in his own room, but my 5-year-old is just not ready yet. He has a few times, but he's a late bloomer in everything—walking, potty training, and talking. We do what works and feels right to us. We are able to snuggle with our little ones this way; they grow so fast. We know we will never regret it! They love it and we do, too. I couldn't bear the thought of making them cry just so they could sleep in their own room. Our children are very secure, just as they should be according to Dr. Sears' books (*4), and they go to sleep right away. The only drawback is that I have to lay down with the 3-year-old and baby for about 15 minutes to get them to sleep, but I would have to nurse the baby anyhow, so it's fine. They go to sleep fine for others on date night too!—*Tina*

♥ During the last year, we've had one big bedroom for all of the children to share, except the baby who co-sleeps with us. Some share double beds, and some build forts and sleep on the floor for long periods of time. In our last house, we had the eldest five sleep in the basement in various arrangements, all in an open area. We like bunk-beds to free up floorspace. We usually have a mattress on floor beside our bed for the little ones to sleep on if they have a bad dream.—*Karol*

How do you find time to care for the physical needs of the baby (like feeding, bathing and potty-training) while meeting the emotional needs of the older ones?

♥ For nursing, I just sit down and do it! I need the rest! With potty-training, they eventually get it. I don't work with them, they just do it one day. I do keep a potty chair out, but I don't take the time to push it. When the older ones were young, I figured they would eventually catch on before they got married, and so far, they all have!—*Sheri*

♥ We've had success with the buddy system for toilet training. The two oldest girls and I take turns bringing the little ones to the toilet. When I nurse the baby, the older kids entertain the younger ones. Nursing really isn't an issue, since I'm right there; they just continue what they were doing before I started nursing.—*Lissa*

♥ To be completely honest, you don't stress out as much about this as your family grows. Plus, the older the children are, the more they understand and can either help or keep busy for a while. I've always explained to the older child how I used to do "this" when he or she was a baby. Some day, the baby will be bigger and I won't have to do it anymore.—*Shannon*

♥ Only by the grace of God! The little ones tend to get my attention more in the morning and during the day whereas the older kids get the evenings. I try to take one or two of the middle children along with me when I run errands so that I can touch base with them.—*Karina*

♥ This gets easier as the older kids get older. My 5-year-old (or even 3-year-old) can hold the baby while I take the 2-year-old (or myself!) to the bathroom. I find the act of nursing very stressful. It makes me anxious, tense, and irritable. I do not like to do it around the other kids. I also can't sleep through it. I take the baby into another room and feed him or her there. I guess I'm blessed to have children who can deal with it if I say, "I'm going to feed the baby. See you in 20 minutes. I'm right next door if you need anything."—*Betsy*

♥ I don't think I really have to find time; those things just become part of the daily routine. The older ones know that they will have to occasionally be patient while I finish something with the younger. I will confess that the baby gets bathed less than the others, but she doesn't get as dirty either!—*Ann*

♥ We succeed mainly by making everything a group effort. If anyone wants attention when I'm nursing, there's plenty of room for them to cuddle up. Sometimes we read a book, too. If I need space, I ask them to go take out their dolls! The older kids *love* helping with anything involving the younger ones, so even potty training is exciting. They take a lot of pride in the others' progress when they are directly involved.—*Kate*

♥ Nursing and potty training are the hardest to do at once. My oldest can help anyone who needs to use the potty immediately, but I try to make sure there are no emergencies while I'm nursing. I include my oldest helpers in what I'm doing, so caring for the little ones is a joint effort that gives the big ones and me bonding time as well. Also, during nap time, I make sure to be with the older ones. That was hard for me at first. I was used to having nap time to myself. But time with children is so fleeting in the whole scheme of life.—*Amy*

♥ One good thing about a large family is that each child has to learn about preferring others and being patient as they wait their turn. Since we as parents can't do everything at once, there are many times when older ones have to wait while the baby is being attended to. Then, later on, the little one has to wait while the attention is on the older one. Breastfeeding babies is much more conducive to multi-tasking than any other method of infant feeding! I can quite easily nurse my baby and read a story to an older child at the same time, or kiss an owie, or play a game, or supervise schoolwork, or even hold a bigger child on my knees!—*Sarah*

♥ That's the daily miracle! You "do what you're given to do" from moment to moment. Live one day at a time and rely on the grace of God!—*Reba*

♥ Many times I would read to the older kids while I was nursing the baby. Sometimes, I moved the potty chair into the kitchen so it would be close while we were doing other things. I usually bathed the baby in a baby tub while the older ones were in the big tub. When he or she was older, they would bathe together with one or two older ones.—*Betty*

Editor's Note: I have used Betty's "moving potty chair" trick many-a-time. At first, I thought it would be strange to have a potty chair in any other room of the house besides the bathroom. But after awhile, I got used to it. The chair follows us around the house during those first few days of potty-training. That way, I don't forget to offer it to the toddler, nor do I have to move to supervise its use.

♥ I have to have a schedule. If I don't, things get too rushed. When I am nursing, I have younger ones doing something in the same room that I don't have to help them do.—*Mery*

♥ I have to make the infant the priority, as his actual life depends on me. I try to read while I nurse, and wear the baby when I can. We have different seats around the house for the baby to watch the older children and me.—*Diana*

♥ The more children we have, the more everyone learns to wait a little to have their needs met. Sometimes, the baby has to wait, and sometimes it's the older ones. I try to predict needs and account for other needs accordingly. For instance, if a diaper needs changing, I give a school assignment that can be done independently for a few minutes. If I need to nurse, I bring the toddler up on the couch to read with me at the same time. We often spend time reading with a toddler on the potty and a younger one on my lap sitting on the bathroom floor!—*Laurie*

♥ Potty training is not something I stress about much. They get it when they are ready and all of mine have potty trained before they were 4. My oldest daughter and I do a Bible study once a week after the kids are in bed. I try to take my older ones with me when I run errands and my husband is home, so I get some alone time with them.—*Harriet*

♥ The first year is always hard, but I use my Ergo (*5) a lot! My baby is 1 now and all the other children entertain him a lot! I will nurse while on the computer or talking to a friend on the phone. Potty training is hard for us because we have no bathroom downstairs! I can't get upstairs and nurse at the same time. So, my 3-year-old has regressed! She was potty trained a year ago, but is back in pull-ups during the day!—*Tina*

Do you feel that it is important to have alone time with each child each day?

♥ In my little dream world, it would be nice, but that would take all day! So as the Lord opens doors, I take the opportunities; but it's definitely not daily alone time.—*Sheri*

♥ I don't think that "alone time" is always needed, as long each they feel they are getting enough attention in general. They take turns having a breakfast date with Daddy every Monday. They alternately run errands with me, as well. They have voiced how they enjoy this rotating set up.—*Lissa*

♥ As ideal as that would be, there just aren't enough hours in a day! Really though, because we homeschool, and I'm around them all day, I feel like I'm pretty on top of what's going on in their lives. I can sense when one has a bigger need, and I'll make a point of doing something alone with that child.—*Karina*

♥ No. Usually our kids get alone time with one of us once a week. And sometimes "alone time" means just one kid and the baby, much like Mom and Dad's "alone time" with each other often includes the babe. On birthdays, the birthday kid gets to stay up late with Mom and Dad and drink cocktails. Alone time is nice, but I don't think big family parents should beat themselves up over it. This is a social construct that the mainstream culture uses against "breeders." Did Mary, Laura, Carrie, and Grace get alone time every day? How about all those Sowerby kids, or the Five Little Peppers? Of course not.—*Betsy*

♥ Not especially. All of our children are very self-confident. I believe it stems from their security at home. As they grow older and more independent, I might have to seek them out for individual time more. The older girls both know that they just need to ask for anything, even time with Mom and Dad, and we'll make it happen. I've also stressed with them that any time something is bothering them at school, or if there's something they don't understand, they can ask me, and they won't get in trouble. This worked out well when my daughter asked about the four-letter "S" word last year! We explained what it meant, why it's wrong to use it, and then contacted the teacher about it. All was fine.—*Kate*

♥ Remember, you will never be everything to everybody. Accept that. God is the only one who can fully meet each of our children's needs, so don't feel guilty when you realize somebody's needs got missed. Trust God to fill in all the areas where you fall short. He's a great fixer-upper! With a large family, the busiest time is when you have three or four little ones, especially if your children come at about 18–24 month intervals. After that, they truly become helpful and somewhat self-sufficient.—*Karol*

♥ I feel it is important to connect with each child individually each day, to look in their eyes and communicate how special they are. They are not just one of the bunch. But that can be done while prepping dinner together or running errands together. It doesn't have to be unnatural.—*Amy*

♥ I don't think its realistic to expect some Hallmark moment with each child each day. An individual hug and kiss, definitely. Individual time can include diaper changes, potty training, and chore demonstrations. Not glamorous, but necessary.—*Reba*

♥ Sure. It's not always long or significant. However, I try to snatch little bits of snuggles, tickling, reading, and hugs with each of them every day and throughout the day.—*Laurie*

♥ I don't think it's always possible, but a good goal to have.—*Harriet*

♥ Yes, it is. I let my children have one day a week to stay up 15 minutes past their bedtime in order to have one-on-one time with me. We play a game, read, talk, or whatever they want to do.—*Lyn*

♥ Sure, it's important! Is it possible? I believe in teachable moments! I believe in balance, too! If your son is asking you to read a book to him—take advantage of 5 minutes and do it! If your daughter wants to join in—let her! You've just given undivided attention to both. Your son doesn't think mom has to be alone with him for it to count. It counts! I don't agree with all the psychobabble out there that says you need to spend at least one hour a week with each child! How ridiculous! Show me where God says that in the Bible? God gave these beautiful children to us and He will provide the opportunities and time they each need, whether that's 5 minutes or 5 hours! Know your children and their needs individually. Don't try to make it fair; just do what you can! Have balance though, and don't sacrifice yourself entirely either. Your kids can manipulate you if you give in too much. Balance is the key and teachable moments are great!—*Tina*

♥ This might be great idea, but isn't usually practical. Learn their love languages (*6). Some just need words of affirmation or a loving physical touch while others need chunks of time.—*Karol*

Do your children have overlapping social groups? How do you arrange for all of them to see friends or have friends come over?

♥ Friends are always over! The age-range of the visitors is wide. Our children are socialized vertically (with many age groups), rather than the way it's traditionally done in schools, which is horizontally. In the end, they will encounter more real-life experiences being socialized vertically. We are helping to prepare them for the real world in this way!—*Lissa*

♥ We've had some play-dates. I don't enjoy them simply because I am very antisocial myself. Basically, if someone asks, we accept and then return the favor. I do not seek out additional complications since my kids already have plenty of people with whom to play right here.—*Betsy*

♥ We usually have family play-dates with other families that have children of similar ages. It's fun for the moms and the kids!—*Ann*

♥ Since they attend a small school, my daughters have about the same social group. We allow them to go to friends' houses when we know and are comfortable with the adults in the home; there are several families in our church that we trust completely. I try to take everyone up on their invitations. Whenever the kids ask, and I think I can handle it, we have a friend over for the day, or overnight. I guess I don't make a specific effort to arrange these things, but when the opportunity knocks, we usually try to make it work.—*Kate*

♥ We greatly limit the amount of peer interaction our children have. We do have like-minded friends with children of similar ages. We try to socialize in a family setting like dinner, picnics, or family parties. We don't drop our kids off anywhere. We do joint lessons with other friends, such as sign language classes and violin lessons. We want our children to be best friends with each other. We find that a "that's my friend, that's your friend" mentality doesn't support that. People are not welcome in our house if it becomes a case of preferring some siblings and excluding others. However, because I am always around I'll know if a younger sibling needs to be corralled (like if he's wrecking the board game everyone is playing)!—*Amy*

♥ The best friends for our children to have have been given to them within our family unit. We really encourage that. It might sound like restriction, bondage, or whatever. But it has the benefit that we are seldom restricted to our vehicle, being a taxi driver for our children!—*Karol*

♥ All of our children's friends have been met through families in our charter school. They see each other at different classes, field trips, or play-dates. Our rule is that you have to plan for play-dates; there are no spontaneous get-togethers. This eliminates my own feeling guilty about saying no.—*Christy*

♥ We do not allow sleep-overs, and play-dates are supervised so nothing "funny" happens while I am unaware. I listen to the conversations when we have teens over.—*Mitzi*

♥ Our children's friends are children in other large families. They see friends at church and park day with our homeschool group, and at Awana. We occasionally try to schedule play-dates with friends, but that is not our focus right now.—*Harriet*

♥ Church, church events, and after church meals are such are a great source of fellowship for all of us. We also try to regularly invite other families over to our home for dinner and visiting. During the weekdays, we occasionally get together with other homeschoolers at a museum, park, or in our home.—*Laurie*

♥ The kids can each have a friend over twice a month.—*Mery*

♥ As a very social person myself, I've kept the children's social circle's quite full and, yes, right now they are all overlapping. They're not old enough yet to go alone to see friends, but I'm sure the time will come soon!—*Sarah*

♥ Our kids interact with kids of the parents we're interacting with! We have our "best friends" that we see at least once a week; they have eight cousins that live close by; they do have friends at church that they see occasionally outside of church. Sometimes, we might swap a boy for a girl with the cousins!—*Dana*

How do the older children feel about taking on so much responsibility with managing younger siblings, and how do the younger ones feel about having to obey the older ones?

♥ Some love it, but others don't and view responsibility as a chore. I have tried the Buddy System, but right now it isn't working very well in our house. I don't want to force it, because it only causes sibling rivalry, so I don't require them to help their buddy at the moment. I would like to change that, but I need to see heart changes first. I would love to have everyone paired up with a buddy eventually, but I don't know if that will ever work for our family.—*Tina*

♥ My older ones seem to take pride in helping out the little ones. I've also learned to be mindful that when I have a job to give out, I give it to the youngest one capable of doing it. This really helps to prevent "oldest child burnout" as the more complex jobs get saved for the older ones and the littler ones feel important doing the easier and more mundane jobs.—*Sarah*

> **Editor's Note:** What a great idea to assign tasks to the youngest child possible! I'm sure my oldest is thankful I've been implementing it!

♥ It is part of the privilege of belonging to a large family. You help one another. But I try to be careful not to "expect" too much. I try to encourage them that it helps me when they help with the younger children. Occasionally, when I sense a bit of whining, I'll simply say, "It's all right. I'll do it myself." This usually seems to take care of things pretty quickly. Let the Holy Spirit do the work. Just be careful not to come across as miffed.—*Karina*

♥ We have "indoctrinated" our children that we must all work together for the well-being of our family. Everybody must do their part. Our oldest two daughters are now 21 and 22. They have always been my right-hand helpers, and much responsibility fell on them when I was pregnant with another, or recovering from a birth. We have managed to convince the children that another brother or sister is positive, although there is more work. Our family verse is "Whatsoever your hand findeth to do, do it with all of your might as working for the Lord, not for men." Perhaps because of this, our eldest daughters seem to be the favorites of their bosses in the workplace!—*Karol*

How do you respond to others who say that large families are poor stewards of the earth because of carbon footprints and garbage output?

♥ I would say that large families tend to recycle more as far as clothes and other necessities. They eat at home and cook from scratch, so there is less waste. I think large families value and take care of what they have because they learn to share it and think of others.—*Betty*

♥ Environmental critics: No one in our family has flown for three years, and that was just Dad on one domestic round trip. I can't remember the last air travel before that. Most days my car doesn't leave the garage and Dad walks to work. We don't have any beef at home, CAFO or otherwise. We harvest and process our own local game and fish and don't buy produce all summer long. I line dry whenever the weather is good enough. Still want to argue?—*Betsy*

♥ I have not had to deal with hearing this in person from anyone. But, if I did, I don't think it would phase me much. I'm raising my children to be good stewards of what God has given us. I believe my children will be much more balanced in making decisions about how and what needs to be done in order to care for our planet, which is what I don't see in many of the environmentalists. I could go on for hours about this one because it touches so many areas in life in the modern world, but suffice it to say the critics are just another sounding brass and tinkling cymbal blowing in the wind.—*Sheri*

♥ Responding to earth worshipers: I ignore it. Where would I begin? It's mostly non-believer's nonsense, so there are bigger issues to discuss with those folks. For a Christian with that attitude, it is easy to simply point to Scripture. All of nature is groaning and rotting away—with or without my help. I just do what I'm given to do and God set before me the task of bearing and rearing children. Besides, maybe one of my many children will come up with a new energy source! Ha!—*Reba*

♥ Environmental critics are people who worship the creation instead of the Creator. Therefore, Biblically, I don't think it's an issue. My doctor has 7 kids, and he had a few patients that criticized him; his response was that his children would contribute more to the world than they would ever take away.—*Dana*

♥ I don't really pay attention to the environmental critics. I homeschool and we don't travel a lot, so we really only take the big van on Sunday to church in the morning. The majority of the time, we drive just a few children around in a compact, efficient car. I cook a few meals at a time and freeze them, so I don't waste energy. We are very big on making sure electronics and lights are turned off when we leave rooms.—*Laurie*

Chapter Four

When You *Really* Need a Break

"She extends her hand to the poor,
Yes, she reaches out her hands to the needy. ...
She makes tapestry for herself;
Her clothing is fine linen and purple. ...
Charm is deceitful and beauty is passing,
But a woman who fears the LORD, she shall be praised."
Proverbs 31:20,22,30

The saying goes that "if Mama ain't happy, nobody's happy." No one can deny the truth that a content mother sets the emotional tone for the whole family. But, busy mothers rarely get the "time to themselves" that the world says they need. How can they ever manage to have enough love in their tanks to spill over? The mothers below dispel the myth that taking care of oneself requires an excessive amount of time. Read on for tips that will leave you refreshed and ready to give. Or, if that fails, then read on for a reality check: sometimes you can't "have it all."

When do you take care of your own hygiene?

♥ Wake up early, get done quickly!—*Shannon*

♥ Ideally, before everybody is up. Realistically, after everybody else is dressed and fed. Really bad day, when Dad gets home.—*Betsy*

♥ Whenever I can, sometimes not as often as I would like. I am usually really happy if I get to brush my teeth two times a day and brush my hair!—*Ann*

♥ If I'm going to the gym or doing errands that day, I get up a little earlier than the kids. I'll have my shower, sometimes put on makeup, and get into clean clothes. On Sundays I need to get up super early, because I like to be really put-together for church. Evenings, after everyone's in bed, are my chance to soak in the bathtub. I probably do that two or three nights per week.—*Kate*

♥ In the morning or it doesn't happen! My dear daughter, 10, is usually up and helps with the baby.—*Dana*

♥ I do it in the morning, while kids are eating breakfast. Some days I am unable to get a shower in the morning, so I do it when Dad's getting the kids ready for bed.—*Sharon*

♥ When my eldest were still little, it was whenever my dear husband was around and I could jump in the shower. Then, when some of the children were old enough to babysit, I took a few minutes for myself. At all stages of family life, I've enjoyed a quiet hot bath at night when the little ones are all in bed. Especially the night my Above Rubies magazine arrives, I steal away to the tub to read!—*Karol*

♥ I do it in the early morning because once the day starts, the time is gone, and I like privacy.—*Lissa*

♥ I have some time after everyone is in bed, plus I get up an hour before everyone else in order to have time to get myself together and pray before starting the day.—*Lyn*

♥ First thing in the morning, we all get ready. The children dress and brush teeth. I shower, brush my teeth, etc. I find that if I don't do it right away in the morning, it is difficult to find the time later or I'm rushing to get ready when we need to go somewhere. We have a stool in our bathroom so that the little ones can brush their teeth (they love to do this for a long time if I leave a small drip of water going) and we also have a bottom drawer full of their books and toys that they may play with while I get dressed, wash up, and all that.—*Laurie*

♥ I shower at night. Sometimes that means calling Daddy away from the computer to manage the baby for awhile!—*Reba*

What types of "beauty routines" did you do before you had children that you can't continue now? How do you handle this?

♥ None really. I do splurge once in a while and have my eyebrows waxed. I figure I'm worth it.—*Sheri*

♥ Honestly, I don't even remember. I've managed to keep the ones that are most important: showering, shaving, painting nails.—*Lissa*

♥ I used to have an expensive hair style, went tanning, and spent much more time applying make-up. I handle this with a much more "natural" look. Simple hair cut, low maintenance style, and less make up. No tanning—it's bad for the skin!—*Shannon*

♥ Keep things basic. Have a hair style that is attractive and that suits you, but that doesn't take lots of time.—*Karina*

♥ I'm pretty low maintenance. I spend less time trying on clothes, but that's about the only change. I should floss more. As long as you don't want to wear makeup, do anything complicated to your hair, or paint your nails, kids won't cramp your style too much. My recommendation to all moms: get a nail buffer. You can do your nails while you nurse, and they'll be so smooth and shiny!—*Betsy*

♥ Thankfully I didn't really have any, so I don't feel bad about not getting to do them.—*Ann*

♥ I pretty much have the same routine. I bathe or shower once a day. I shave twice a week (my legs, not my face)! I use face mask every couple of weeks and moisturize. I think it's important to feel (and smell) good, because when I feel bad about myself, I'm more cranky and irritable!—*Kate*

♥ I never really had a beauty routine. Simple and natural works best for me! It is nice to have a pedicure every few months, and is something I have tried to do this past year. I had my nails done for about a year several years ago. It was a nice treat, but not a necessary one.—*Janet*

♥ I used to be a cosmetologist and have every product out there. Alas, I married a man with allergies, so that greatly limited the products I could use. He also likes long hair. So, now, I wear my hair longer, throw it up in a clip, and am good to go. Everything for me takes five minutes. Doing my girls' hair, braiding and such, takes much longer than my own routine!—*Amy*

♥ I was never one to do my make-up, but I do it even less now. Sleep is more important, so it's not directly the kids' fault! I try to do my make-up if I'm going to be with my husband, but no, I don't shave as often as I would like to, or as often as he would like, either! I only wash my hair every other day, and I try to blow dry it because it looks better for the second day!—*Dana*

♥ I've been pretty low maintenance my whole life. I do shower less now, though. That is partly because in Central Asia, we often didn't have water when I was ready to shower.—*Christy*

♥ I spent more time caring for my face. I probably curled my hair more often. Now, I just do it for special occasions. My husband likes my hair straight so that's okay with him! I don't mind. It takes me about 10 minutes to get myself ready in the morning.—*Tina*

♥ I get my hair done once every six weeks or so to be attractive for my husband.—*Lissa*

♥ I don't know that my routine is much different than before, but I've learned how to make it quicker. I wash my hair a little less frequently than I used to and I often fail to wash my face at night anymore. But, I can't say it's any big deal for me. It just doesn't make sense to spend too much time on those kinds of things most days. I never shave my legs anymore; I haven't for many years and I certainly don't think it's gross. I do manage to control my eyebrows a few times a year. I've learned how to spend a shorter amount of time getting ready, and still look decent. And then on special occasions I go all out; my husband really notices!—*Laurie*

♥ I don't do anything differently. I make sure and take care of myself; my kids need to see that I care about myself and that I know I am important, too.—*Mery*

♥ Curling irons, blow-dryers and lots of make-up are out. I have short hair and use some gel. Foundation and mascara are often my only make-up.—*Reba*

♥ I've always been one to keep things simple, so I haven't changed much since having children. I haven't ever worn make-up (and my husband actually prefers it this way!), so that helps. I have really long hair that I only wash once a week, so I've made it a habit that when I wash my hair I shave my legs at the same time, since I'm having a longer shower anyways. Otherwise, I'm in and out of the shower in two minutes or less. When I need to have my longer showers, the children are always good about playing in the play room on their own until I'm done and sometimes the baby climbs in the shower with me.—*Sarah*

Do you have time to exercise, besides running after the children?

♥ I try to at least do toning exercises. Also, at different times I have belonged to a women's work-out circuit. This has toning machines set up in a circle. You spend 90 seconds at each machine, then move on to the next. Each machine tones/strengthens a different part of your body. There are about 15 machines, and you go around twice. There are other machines at these places too, and I usually did 20 minutes on an elliptical machine, as well. I've also cycled at times. It just depends on where I'm at with being pregnant or nursing a baby. It's very high on my priority list to stay in shape as much as possible, as I've seen how weight issues get out of control with mothers who've had many children. It affects so many other areas of our lives if we're out of shape. But it is a struggle to keep things in control.—*Karina*

♥ If I were honest, I'd say, "Yes, I could make time to exercise." It's just not high on my priority list (or my "favorite thing to do" list). I go in phases of interest. I'll do great for a while and then fizzle out. —*Shannon*

♥ I have occasionally worked out a schedule with Dad so that I can go out and run, but this only works if the weather cooperates and I'm up for it. We can make time, but I have to *really* want it, and I usually don't want it enough!—*Betsy*

♥ Until my third child came along, I made sure to do a workout video at least three times per week, and our family would frequently take walks together when the weather was right. Once our third arrived, I received a gym membership as a Mother's Day gift from my husband. He told me that he was trying to decide which I'd like more, someone to help me clean or a gym membership, and he chose correctly! I can't even begin to tell you how positive this has been for me, even though I'm not a sports person! I really had to work hard to get the weight off after that third child! So, on Mondays, Wednesdays, and Fridays, the two youngest and I leave for a morning workout class after I've sent the older two kids to school. I'm back by 9:30 a.m. and excited to get on with the work I've planned for the day.—*Kate*

♥ It's always a nice thought, but since my third child, it is something I have not done regularly. Aside from walks with the family after dinner or swimming now and then, chasing the children *is* my exercise!—*Janet*

♥ I run every day on the treadmill for two or three miles. I usually run sometime in the afternoon. My oldest watches the 1-year-old and the rest play or roller-skate in the basement. I shower afterward with the baby playing in my room. The rest of the kids are assigned a task. I find assigning jobs works *really* well in keeping children busy and not fighting with each other! However, I haven't run since I got pregnant. Now, I nap instead!—*Amy*

♥ I don't make the time for it. We go for walks together, but I should add in some stretching and weight-lifting at home. We are going to budget for some outdoor exercise/play equipment, like bikes and helmets or a parachute and balls.—*Dana*

♥ Now that my oldest is able to babysit for a while, I do. Maybe 2 or 3 times a week I take a walk by myself.—*Christy*

♥ I have little time for it, which is why my mid-section is suffering!—*Sharon*

♥ I just joined Curves 2 months ago. I try to go at least 3 times a week. At first, I had a certain time I went, but life is too unpredictable, so now I go when I can squeeze in 40 minutes away, usually when my dear husband gets home and dinner is in the oven, or just after dinner.—*Tina*

♥ I have to make time. I walk with a friend early one morning a week. I try to attend a class at the local YMCA with my husband. We attend late afternoon or evening classes. The Y's childcare opens around 4 p.m. which is about when our school schedule ends for the day. When the kids were younger, I went to a morning class and they would take their school work to do in the childcare room while my eldest went with me to class. Now our schedule is a bit different and I don't find that that time of day works for me anymore.—*Harriet*

♥ I try to make exercise a priority. I feel better, I look better, I sleep better, and I definitely have more energy when I exercise regularly! When pregnant, I workout 2 to 4 times per week. I alternate between strength training and cardiovascular exercise. When I'm a few months post-partum, I step it up a notch. I usually workout 5 or 6 times a week and work quite a bit harder in an effort to lose baby weight and get in better shape between babies. I keep it short: 20 or 30 minutes per workout. We have equipment set up in our basement with a great toy room on the other side of the room. The children can play or watch a short video while I exercise. Sometimes, it's hard to justify making this a priority, but I think in the long run it is good for my children to have a healthy, fit, and energetic mom! And I know it is a boost to my marriage to make efforts in this area, and that is definitely good for my children!—*Laurie*

♥ I could if I got up a little earlier, but we do take walks as a family. —*Mery*

♥ I aim for a 30 minute routine 3 times a week, but often only manage once a week. But, I do garden, mow the lawn, and shovel snow.—*Reba*

♥ Yes, but most of the time I am too lazy to do it. Every morning, though, after the children get up, we read the Bible and then take a 2 mile walk before breakfast.—*Lyn*

Editor's Note: Taking a 2-mile walk before breakfast does *not* sound lazy to me!

♥ I do my best to keep up a short regular routine for core muscle strengthening and overall stretching. It's been my goal to keep my abdominal muscles in tip-top shape, as I've always wanted to have a large family and want to keep my muscles strong to bear a lot of children. I work really hard post-partum to get back to the shape I was in previously. In the summer, I do a lot of biking and walking with the children. For a few months between each child, I've taken up running. (I have to take it easy during pregnancy.) I have two flights of stairs in my house, so I run a lot of stairs everyday too. I think keeping active helps to build energy for my job as a mom. I certainly get a lot of activity in my days playing with my children as well, especially in the summertime.—*Sarah*

> **Editor's Note:** In addition to all of the exercise ideas listed above, I've heard lots of good things from mom friends about the T-Tapp system (*1). It's supposed to pack all of the benefits of a long workout into 10 or 15 minutes a day.

How close are your closest friends? How often do you hear from them or get together?

♥ Not very and not often.—*Sheri*

♥ We e-mail often and see each other on Sundays and possibly for a play-date once a month.—*Lissa*

♥ I have several close friends and one best friend. We used to talk nearly every day, but with our busy lives, it has dwindled down to once every couple of weeks. But we re-connect easily.—*Shannon*

♥ I'm not one who needs a lot of close friends. We have couples we spend time with, but they have large families as well, so it's more often that we're together as families than that I'm with one or two close friends.—*Karina*

♥ I have a group blog with two of my closest friends since we live far from each other. We try to arrange our vacations to incorporate visits with friends' families.—*Betsy*

♥ My sister is three hours away and we get together once or twice a month. I walk regularly with my other closest friend, so we see each other quite a bit!—*Ann*

♥ I am very close to my sisters, but only get to see them once a year. I talk with my closest sister at least 3 hours a week! I also use Facebook to keep in contact with all of them. As for friends in the area, I have some good friends, but we don't get together often. I see them more at church and school functions. I might "get together" with someone once in 2 or 3 months. That was a very hard adjustment because I got married and moved straight out of college where there was always someone to have fun with! And the adjustment was so much harder because our church was all retirees at first! But as our church situation has changed, and I've met other mothers through the kids' activities, that has gotten easier. But being far away from my kindred spirits (my sisters and best friends) is an ongoing challenge that I am learning how to live with.—*Kate*

♥ There is a time and season for everything under the sun! Some seasons are ebb and some flow for getting together with friends. As a homeschooler, once a quarter we have a "Moms Gathering" where we get together at someone's home for dinner, encouragement and sharing on a topic. Locally, there are several moms that I speak with or see from time to time and thank the Lord for that time. I have some friends that I don't see or speak with as often and it makes it all the sweeter when those times happen. Letter writing or dropping a card in the mail helps to stay connected.—*Janet*

> **Editor's Tip:** I love this idea from Janet! Who doesn't love to get the mail and see a note from a friend? I find keeping a few note-cards handy on my desk lets me quickly write a note of encouragement or a Bible passage to a friend and stick it in the mail when there's a moment of time between schoolwork or helping the children. Now, where are those stamps I just bought?!

♥ My "best friend" has been my friend since fourth grade! She is so special to me. She only lives a few blocks away, and we talk almost every day and get together once or twice a week. Sometimes, we do school together. When I had the baby, she kept my other 4 kids for 3 nights and even did some school with them! What a blessing! My husband really likes it when I spend time with certain friends, because he knows they encourage me in the Lord and as a wife and mom, and I'm in a better mood afterward!—*Dana*

♥ Right now, my closest girl friend lives in China! But my husband is my dearest friend. I am good at emailing friends because I can do that late at night, or in little snatches, a sentence here or there. Phone conversations don't go so well that way! I meet with some friends weekly during a sign-language class and violin lessons; others, I don't see as often. Maybe monthly?—*Amy*

♥ Our very best friends just had their seventh dear child! We go through seasons where we see them often, then go for months during the cold season when we might not see them at all. Usually, part of our family would at least see part of their family on a regular basis. My other girlfriends and I keep in touch often on email as it fits our individual situations. We no longer live near each other so we talk less on the phone and obviously don't see each other in person. We are 4 time zones apart!—*Karol*

♥ We are not as close as when we were younger. I probably talk to one friend on the phone a day and get together with one friend a week either as a play date, class, or out to dinner. I'm in a moms' group that meets two times a month at a restaurant with no kids. Also, we are in a co-op and we have monthly meetings just for moms.—*Tina*

♥ I have a prayer partner who is essential and I trust her completely. —*Mitzi*

♥ I have some local friends, but others are very far away. I hardly see the ones that don't live nearby. My dearest local friend and I try to meet at least one time a month for coffee and chatting.—*Harriet*

♥ This is certainly a hard question to answer. Some friends are far away, and we only see them every few years and speak on the phone a couple times a year. Others are here in town and we see them several times per week (many at our weekly worship service) and talk with them often as they become entwined in our lives. It also depends greatly on what is happening in our lives. There are seasons where we are blessed with much time with friends and other seasons where busyness, sickness, or weather keep us apart for a while. I do spend time differently with girlfriends than with my husband. If I brainstormed and confided in my husband about every household and child-related issue that I do with certain women, he would be absolutely bored to tears. And probably much less patient and willing to really talk about the important issues that we need to discuss and solve together. I definitely have a couple of solid women friends who help me to figure out and clarify some problems/household function issues/even marital glitches *before* I go to my husband with these things. That way I've already gotten beyond the emotions and such and am ready to approach him with a more consolidated and rational discussion— which I believe is a huge help to our communication!—*Laurie*

♥ My closest friends are my homeschool co-op friends and friends at church. In the past year, my husband and I started getting together with another couple for wine in the evenings once or twice a week because we finally have kids old enough to manage things when the little ones are in bed. So, we do get some adult time in the evenings! In the past, we got together with another homeschool family every weekend: Friday or Sunday, whichever would work for both of us. If it was Friday, we played a game or watched a movie together.—*Reba*

♥ My only sister, my mom, and about five other women are my closest friends. I talk to them each about once a week. I have a lot of friends and acquaintances. I often take my children and meet friends at the playgrounds or go for walks together. We also have friends over for meals quite often in the summertime or meet up with friends for picnics. I use email to keep in touch with a few of my friends. I also have one childhood friend with whom I regularly exchange handwritten letters.—*Kimi*

What hobbies are large-family friendly?

♥ Having babies is my hobby! We have visited the state capital on behalf of homebirth. We sometimes help at local activities with clean-up.—*Sheri*

♥ Blogging and writing. I do these while the kids do school work or in the afternoon while the little ones are napping and other children are outside or playing.—*Lissa*

♥ I like reading, scrapbooking, and drawing. I try to do these things with the children—they love them, too. But sometimes, I also get together with my friends to scrapbook (without the children). I like reading before bed to relax. I also like to volunteer for many great causes. I'm the family coordinator for my husband's Marine Corps unit. This is nearly a full-time job. I love to help in church and school. I do have a hard time saying no and often stretch myself too thin. Even though my kids don't actually volunteer with me, I think they see the rewards of helping out.—*Shannon*

♥ I do enjoy scrapbooking, but that tends to be a twice-a-year two-day get-away that I do on my own. My older daughters also enjoy this with me. We all love sewing. And I love trying new things to cook, but that also doesn't happen too often with time being of the essence. I also love gardening and this year "hired" my 11-year-old daughter to be my gardener. It has been great to involve her and has given us one-on-one time together.—*Karina*

♥ I really don't have any. There just isn't enough uninterrupted time in my day. I don't think this is really healthy, but I don't know that always looking for time to do something I don't have time for would make me happy either. Blogging is about as close as I get. However, I do as many church-related activities as I can, and people around here understand that the babies go where I go.— *Betsy*

♥ My hobbies are cooking and baking. The kids sit on the counter if they want to watch, and I let them measure and mix ingredients if I'm not in too much of a rush. I like to sew, often with someone on my lap! Also, reading, which I try not to do during the day or I'll neglect the kids. Music is another hobby. The girls love to dance to whatever I'm playing on the piano. Traveling is also a good family hobby and we all enjoy the adventures that come with nonstop road trips. In addition, I volunteer at church and school whenever I can. Our whole family goes to choir on Wednesday nights because I direct. Other times, like when I need time practicing organ alone, I will go when my husband is home. If it's a school activity, such as a field trip or Valentine's Day party, I bring the younger kids along, and the teachers and students think it's great. —*Kate*

♥ I enjoy scrapbooking and have included my children in that hobby. They create a "yearbook" each year of the learning opportunities they have had. This year, I am hosting three "yearbook" classes so other children can create and work on their "yearbook." The classes are two hours long, with the first 30 or 45 minutes devoted to instruction time and then the remainder of the class is their time to work on their individual books. A light snack is served at the end. This allows a time for them to learn new ideas, create an individualized "yearbook" that is designed by them and a time of fellowship with other homeschoolers. I also love organizing and bookmaking. I enjoy helping friends with scheduling and organizing. I have a wonderful husband who gives me time to do these things, and scheduling, again, helps in this area. Also, we volunteer through ministry at church—for family, neighbors, and friends. My children are included when preparing meals for other people, and sometimes in ministry at the church. —*Janet*

♥ I scrapbook. That's easy to do with the kids. They all love stickers and die cuts and cool paper. My son loves to work on my

husband's old truck with him. My big girls and I will read together.
—*Amy*

♥ It used to be scrapbooking, but I couldn't keep up. Now, I crochet with my oldest three daughters. I also read and am studying to be a childbirth educator.—*Christy*

♥ I crochet, sew, embroider, read, and do other things, too. I will be teaching my daughter to do the crafty stuff as she is able. We all love to read and spend a lot of time reading out loud. The children who can read take turns, too.—*Ann*

♥ I don't have time or ambition for hobbies these days. Someday, I will get back into doing them. However for now, I'm happy taking the time to be with the children.—*Sharon*

♥ I don't have hobbies anymore! After my fourth child, they went out the window—ha! They became low on the priority list of what needed to be done. Seriously! I used to quilt and sew. I painted our whole house when we first moved and enjoyed it. I used to ride horses. I still read some novels, but that's about it. There is just no time and it's too stressful to try.—*Tina*

♥ Hobbies are similar to friendships in that there are seasons of opportunity to do this, with children or with friends. There are other seasons when I don't get an opportunity for a particular hobby for many months. With reading and gardening, also, there are seasons of plenty and seasons with hardly any time.—*Laurie*

♥ I used to sew, but don't anymore. I like to "escape" to my garden when I can. I used to do a lot of crafts, but I guess cooking, baking, and laundry are my "hobbies" now, and reading school stuff!—*Reba*

♥ I let my daughters volunteer at the library!—*Mery*

♥ I'm accredited as a Leader for La Leche League (*2). This is something that seems to fit quite easily into our life. I only take my youngest child to meetings since the meetings are in evenings around bedtime. It's easier for me to have only one child to manage when I have leader responsibilities and am trying to reach out to the other moms who come. I have found this to be an amazing way to get into community life here and get to know other moms. LLL also believes in "mother-sized jobs" and working together as a team, so that no one feels overloaded because mothering is upheld as the most important task of each leader. We also like to ride horses and occasionally take my children with me to the ranch where I used to work to teach them to ride. I'm hoping we can find a way to board our own horse, so that we can ride more often. I love music and am teaching piano to my girls. My oldest daughters and I are taking violin lessons together. I like to sketch and paint and I occasionally take up a project, but this is something I would work on after the children are in bed. I'm starting to teach the girls how to paint a little bit with watercolors. I enjoy sewing and I make dresses for my daughters. This is something I can do during the day. I have a big sewing table set up and the biggest girls are learning how to help pin the patterns with me. The little ones love to watch and sit on my lap when I'm sewing. My two biggest girls have little toy ponies with magnets on their feet, so if we ever have pins spill on the floor, they're eager to use their ponies to pick up the pins as quickly as possible so that the baby doesn't get into them. When I'm not working on my project, I close off that area so that the children can't keep "sewing" without me.—*Sarah*

> **Editor's Tip:** I love Sarah's idea of having an area that can be closed-off for leaving projects out. I know I am much more likely to work on a project if I don't have to constantly clean up after myself. It's also nice for the older children to have an area to work on puzzles or Legos that the littler ones can't get into. For us, the area is our guest room that is only seldom used, but I've heard of other families getting creative with closets, porches, and baby-gates.

How do vacations work for your large family?

♥ We don't take elaborate vacations, but we love the mountains and try to save for a trip each year. We rent a house and cook most meals while we are there. Our museum membership has a reciprocal list, so we visit museums in the area that are on the list for free! We visit the historic sites of the area, which is also a cost-effective activity. We have wonderful memories and traditions that have been established from doing this.—*Janet*

♥ We rent condos through eBay or VRBO (*3), which is much cheaper than multiple hotel rooms. We'll bring our own food and eat out once a week while on vacation. We search for coupons ahead of time, or volunteer to listen to a presentation for free tickets to a place such as Sea World.—*Lissa*

♥ Once or twice a year, we go camping. Zoos, water parks, museums, and playgrounds are large-family friendly.—*Shannon*

♥ We do one big vacation a year to visit the grandparents. I'm not sure how large of a family they'll continue tolerating in years to come. We've considered camping, but I'm not keen on the idea of giving up my bed when I'm either pregnant or nursing, which is always!—*Betsy*

♥ A friend lets us use her timeshare property. It's perfect because it's like living in a small house for a week; there's a washer, dryer, full kitchen, the whole nine yards! We spend time hiking, sledding, looking around the town, watching some cable TV, and just being together. I love it. I guess I've learned that when someone offers something like that, take them up on it, because otherwise you'll miss out! Our final luxury is the road trip each year back home. We have to save for gas, but we pack food and drive straight through the night to save money on hotels.—*Kate*

♥ Other than visits to family, we usually take one or two vacations per year. Staying in places with cabins or going camping is usually the best bet. Sometimes, we try to plan vacations where we will have a kitchen available. If possible, we cook ahead and freeze meals or plan to go shopping for meals to prepare once we arrive. I make muffins for easy car food. They're messy, but they fill you up, and you always have to clean the vehicle after a trip anyway!—*Ann*

♥ We like to camp. However, we have outgrown our tent. None of our children want to sleep alone in the other tent, so we'll have to get a bigger one! For food, I make a lot ahead of time. We bake muffins, bread, and pack snack mix to bring along.—*Amy*

♥ We haven't vacationed in a few years, but our last trip was to a Christian music festival. We enjoyed camping and having our own food, but not the "teen culture" of the festival. Another year, we did a "hotel vacation" with museums and sightseeing; hotels aren't that great with small children because the parents are dead tired and the kids are still jumping around. But, most offer a decent breakfast, so you can start your day more quickly. You just have to call around to hotels until they'll work with you. For meals besides breakfast, we pack a lot in coolers.—*Dana*

♥ Most of our married life, we thought we couldn't afford a vacation, so we only traveled to visit extended family. But now, we realize that we are citizens of another Kingdom, so we are renewing our minds with that understanding. Since then, we have actually taken more vacations than ever before. We recently rented a big six-bedroom vacation house with an outdoor swimming pool for two weeks. It turned out to be owned by a Christian fella who gave us a deduction for the second week, and then gave us the long-weekend at the end of our stay for free! We had a very relaxed time with the children, and greatly improved our swimming skills. We also watched a bunch of great Bible teaching DVDs we've been wanting to watch. As for other trips, while driving, we often find a playground for the children to run around at while one of the adults buys groceries like cheese and crackers, sandwich fixings, or fruit. We allow trail-mix and chips and fruit to be eaten while driving. We don't do the restaurant thing very much because it's way too costly, especially for what you get.—*Karol*

♥ We go to my aunt's cabin in the mountains for a week. We also go skiing for a weekend. We go to Disneyland for a week. We budget for what we are going to do in advance. Plan, plan, plan! At Disneyland, we eat breakfast at the hotel, lunch is packed, and dinner is at a restaurant. We eat out a lot on vacation because it's vacation! It's supposed to be fun!—*Tina*

♥ We try to find places with pools and kitchens in the room. Pools are great entertainment and our kids love to swim. Having a kitchen makes it remarkably easier to manage a family! We grocery shop and eat breakfast and one other meal a day at the resort/condo. Then, we go out to eat for one meal a day. This gives us the fun of eating out and feeling like we're having special vacation privileges, but keeps everything more affordable.—*Laurie*

Chapter Five

Learning Time

"She watches over the ways of her household,
And does not eat the bread of idleness."
Proverbs 31:27

The typical stay-at-home mom in America has only three or four years before she sends her child off to a day-institution to be shaped. Families who choose to homeschool, however, have the privilege of passing on their values to their children every hour of the day for nearly two decades! They also take on the additional challenge of balancing the tasks of housekeeping and child-rearing with those of administrator and teacher. But even mothers of many who have chosen to enroll their children in a school still find creative ways of remaining involved in their children's educations. These mothers share their ideas not only for making home and school work together, but also for helping them thrive.

What special considerations are there for parents of big families when choosing an education for their children? How did you make that decision?

♥ I cannot prescribe for others how to decide; I can only tell you what we have chosen to do. I planned to be a teacher and send my kids to the private school where I taught, but God led me to homeschool when my firstborn was only 1 year old. So, we went that direction. When she was 4, I first found out about the concept of charter schools. I got a job as an Education Specialist at a local charter school and enrolled her for kindergarten there. This allowed us to use state funding to pay for the fine arts and get to know other homeschooling families for support. We were blessed that our charter school was founded by Christians and there were many Christian families enrolled. I still work for a charter school, but it's the third one we've been in because the others have closed. But, many of the same families remain. I oversee the homeschooling curriculum and education of 27 students including my own children. My husband wants me to work outside the home, so this is a great compromise. My kids love the interaction. Sometimes, I wish I didn't have to work, but I quickly pray that God will bring back my contentment. I don't want to become bitter towards my husband; I try to be thankful that I am able to work, homeschool, and be a full-time mother.—*Tina*

♥ After reading Deuteronomy 6, there was never a question about where to school. Homeschooling parents have to be committed to doing what the Lord has called them to do, even when there are days that are down-right hard!—*Sheri*

♥ It was a hard choice. I researched homeschooling, but sent my oldest child to a private school. I later found that our public school was the best choice for us. If the local public school wasn't so great, I would definitely consider homeschooling.—*Shannon*

♥ We feel that God has put us in charge of educating our children and we are not to hand over this job to anyone else. Because of homeschooling, we can tailor each child's education to meet their needs. If they excel at something, they move along faster. If they need more help with something, we can slow it down. We just *love* homeschooling and would *never* have it any other way.—*Lissa*

♥ Some parishes with schools can handle it if the pastor's family homeschools. Ours is not one of them, so our kids will attend the Christian Day School school until eighth grade. We plan to homeschool after this for social, financial, and academic reasons. This would be our decision regardless of the number of kids we have.—*Betsy*

♥ I think money is a big consideration for most families, unfortunately. When money's an issue, some families decide that they cannot afford to homeschool (or to send their kids to a private school). We're blessed to have a parochial school in connection with our church. So, it has been an easy decision for us.—*Kimi*

♥ In the event that my husband was called to a church that didn't have a school (and there were no private schools that we could send the kids to), we would homeschool. That decision would be spiritually-based. No way am I letting the public schools get their hands on my kids' minds!—*Kate*

♥ For us, homeschooling has nothing to do with family size. We believe that is the best way for us to disciple our children and teach them the ways of the Lord. But as an added benefit, I get to spend all day with my children. I can't imagine being able to disciple my children effectively from 4 p.m. to 8 p.m. in the evening, factoring in the dinner rush and any after-school activities. God has called *parents* to train and nurture our children, not someone else. What an awesome responsibility!—*Amy*

♥ We lived in a mission field where homeschooling was our best option when our first daughter started school. Knowing we'd be overseas for a good part of our children's educational years has made this best option for us. It has also provided stability for our children during the many moves we've made.—*Christy*

♥ We started homeschooling because my eldest wanted to learn at 4 years old. So, I started teaching her. She had a January birthday, so it would have been even longer before she could have attended school. By then, I didn't want her to leave, she didn't want to leave, and she was past kindergarten knowledge.—*Sharon*

♥ First, I discovered what my educational philosophy was, and then that dictated what we did. We came to the conclusion that God's ideal is for the parents to be the main educators for a family, and that it is best acquired by living our lives alongside our dear children, like Jesus lived alongside with His disciples while he taught them. We don't use text books because we see that as a totally unnatural way to learn anything. Are we busy preparing our children for the world that we see with our eyes? Or are we prepping them to live by means of the unseen world which is the eternal realm?—*Karol*

♥ This was not a hard decision for me. The schools have gotten so bad that there was no way I wanted my children there. Plus, I felt homeschooling them was what God wanted for our family.—*Lyn*

♥ My kids' relationships are so much better with one another because we homeschool. They are together every day. We did a homeschool co-op two days per week last year, but even that time away from each other caused a strain in their relationships.—*Harriet*

♥ It is a big decision. For my husband and me, we both knew even before we met each other than we'd like to homeschool our children someday. Once we had children, we still definitely felt led strongly in that direction. We wanted to be the primary influence in our children's lives especially during the early years. We also wanted the freedom to teach them both a solid biblical foundation and a wealth of other things besides simply academics.—*Laurie*

♥ We are a military family and the stability of home education is a huge consideration when you move every two or three years. Also, we couldn't afford private school with so many children, so we would have had to depend on a state secular education. That has never been an option. I thank God for the freedom and privilege to educate my own children in the Lord.—*Diana*

♥ My oldest daughter was in public school until the third grade. We make the decision to homeschool at that time because she was being exposed to many things against our morals. It could have taken a lifetime to reverse.—*Mery*

♥ I think you need to take into consideration where the child learns best. Some do very well at home, others learn best with other kids. I homeschooled our oldest in kindergarten because there wasn't a school for him to attend. He was distracted easily and I didn't realize how much I needed to repeat things. I don't think I had enough patience. We were very isolated and it would have been better if we had had other families get together with us and encourage us.—*Betty*

♥ I can't imagine *not* homeschooling, but as with much of our lives, we certainly didn't start out with any kind of plan! Our eldest attended Christian Day School for kindergarten and first grade. I was working full-time, and our other son was in day-care. When my husband finished seminary and was accepted at Notre Dame for graduate school, I was pregnant with our third child. Everything changed. I quit working and stayed home, we started homeschooling, and we started our large family. We didn't make really conscious decisions. God just sort of put people and opportunities in our path to help us make those decisions.—*Reba*

♥ I was homeschooled myself and have always wanted to homeschool my children. When I was a young girl, I used to line up my siblings and "teach" them. My husband had no trouble agreeing to this arrangement and supports me fully. We feel that it is primarily our responsibility to teach our children in the Lord. I am thankful to have the opportunity to teach them academic school subjects, as well as God's Word. We also recognize that it is not possible for every family to go this route and each must do what they feel is best for their family.—*Sarah*

♥ We didn't have a big family when we made the decision to homeschool. We felt it was what God wanted us to do. We wanted to teach our children our values. I knew it would be too expensive to send our kids to private school; I think it would be too "expensive" to send them to public school, too, because they would need more and nicer clothes and school supplies and we'd have to pay for their lunches. With homeschooling, though, we own our books and get to reuse them. This is great for larger families!—*Dana*

For those of you who homeschool, how do you balance between your household activities (such as cooking and cleaning) and teaching your children?

♥ We use the Robinson (*1) method—they teach themselves! This frees up time for me to take care of the home.—*Sheri*

♥ Morning chores are done before school, so the house is clean and presentable for unexpected guests. Lunch is made by me while the kids do their morning schoolwork. Afternoon chores are done in preparation for Daddy's homecoming about 45 minutes before he comes home. It's very manageable as long as everyone is on the "same team"!—*Lissa*

♥ Still working on that!—*Ann*

♥ As mentioned earlier, scheduling is a great way to fit everything into the day based on what the Lord has given you and your children to do. I create a block schedule on the computer—color-coding columns for each person in our family. This schedule serves as our guide for the day, knowing the Lord may direct our paths differently. Having a schedule, however, allows us to minister to others when needs arise, welcome an unexpected visitor, or extend hospitality, simply because most days are orderly and productive. A schedule can be rigid or flexible, but it is at least a point to return to when the path is deviated from.—*Janet*

♥ I try to teach my children all of my household activities. They will be parents and spouses one day. That is what I'm training them for. When I include my children in everything I do, our relationship blossoms!—*Amy*

♥ We have a morning school time and an afternoon school time. When both are done, I can start preparing dinner. I try to do laundry in the evening, so the kids can fold it the next day during free time or rest time.—*Dana*

♥ I'm still learning how to do this with six kids. I guess I just make a plan that will work most days and try to stick to it. When there are short school breaks during the day, I work on laundry or other chores. I plan very simple lunches.—*Christy*

♥ Most of my kids' schoolwork is done individually, without my direct instruction. I only have up to an hour a day working with them. Most of the instruction is done between changing diapers, getting food, cleaning messes, doing laundry, etc. Each of my household activities takes very little dedicated time at once. So I do something, then get to a child's work, and so forth.—*Sharon*

♥ I do a lot of multi-tasking and delegating. I am more structured with the kids in the morning hours; when they are done with their primary chores and lessons, then they receive more freedom in the afternoon. The same goes for me. Some days are more free than others.—*Tina*

♥ My children are using a curriculum which consists mostly of them reading various books. There is not a lot that I am needed for. I have plenty of time for the things I need to get done!—*Lyn*

♥ I'm still working on it! It's a constant work in progress. Morning time is usually school time. In the afternoons, I usually do household chores and run errands.—*Harriet*

♥ We try to cook ahead as much as possible and freeze the extras. This allows us to switch between cooking fresh food and utilizing our frozen meals that are quicker to prepare. I supervise some children while they do schoolwork at the kitchen table, which allows me to also work on food preparation. We try to follow a general schedule of chores first, then breakfast, school time, lunch, rest time, extra school (if needed), outdoor time, free time, and finally, errands. This generally allows me some time during the rest hour and the afternoon to work on dinner preparation or my own housekeeping tasks that haven't been completed for the day. —*Laurie*

♥ My husband does all the laundry, and I cook in big batches whenever I get a chance!—*Diana*

Do homeschoolers differentiate between normal family activities and "school" time? If so, how?

♥ We never used to. But now my oldest is in "fourth grade," so I want to spend some time doing "schoolwork" with her. I think that kids can be taught in two categories: the reader and the non-reader. Basically, I want to teach the non-reader to read. And I want to supply the reader with great books. Of course, I realize that math must be taught. But we really don't spend all that much time on formal schooling.—*Amy*

♥ The kids sure do! Unless we've done math and some sort of writing or workbook page, they think we haven't done school! Devotions should always be done, at least six days a week, but we don't consider that school. We don't do any school in the evenings, when Daddy's home, but we could!—*Dana*

♥ They know that they have certain work to do each day. At 10 a.m., we do devotions, history, and science together—My Father's World (*2). Their copied work for math and language arts are in folders. They can do that work throughout the day, as long as it's done by 4 p.m. I help the 6-year-old with his work throughout the day.— *Sharon*

♥ Nope. Life itself is our education and we don't segment it.—*Karol*

♥ Monday through Friday, we do formal schooling between breakfast and lunch. Informal school is after lunch to bedtime. Formal school consists of lessons that are planned—language, reading, math, history, science, and music practice. Informal lessons are unplanned and spontaneous such as puzzles, computer time, educational videos, educational games, playing outside, exploration, writing, free reading, etc. Weekends are totally open and we try to have family time after church, which includes a lot of informal learning since my husband likes to do nature hikes.—*Tina*

♥ No! All day is learning! There is book time, but it has to weave itself in all day around the running of the home. The kids have the school schedule and fill in their assignment sheets as needed.—*Mitzi*

♥ Everything usually goes hand in hand for us.—*Lyn*

♥ Sometimes we do differentiate, like when we do a math workbook or a writing assignment. Lots of other times we just live and learn all the while without even realizing that we're learning things!—*Laurie*

♥ Yes and no. Some children may be finished with their book work, while others are still working. But, we do not have the 8 a.m. to 3 p.m., Monday through Friday attitude.—*Diana*

♥ Not really. All time in our home is learning and family time, but we do have certain times for school. When my husband is home in the afternoon, we try to be done with all chores so we can spend time with him.—*Mery*

♥ We do the "school at home" approach. During the school year, we have regular school hours. I need the summer off! We also have mid-December through Epiphany off, and usually Holy Week.—*Reba*

Do you have schedules for things like computer time or piano practice?

♥ Each child is allowed 1 1/2 hours of computer time per week. They each have a day of the week for that. Piano is open for free play. Some days, a few of them play a lot and other days they don't touch it.—*Sheri*

♥ Yes and no. Once seatwork is completed, they take turns doing their typing. No one eats lunch until seatwork and typing are done. If we're behind (which is rare), we'll finish up after lunch. Guitar practice is done after school work (which is usually after lunch.)—*Lissa*

♥ No computer games. Period. The computer is used as a tool in our home. Children complete music practice before going outside to play.—*Karina*

♥ Yes, they all have a time when they practice. They are only allowed on the computer for 20 minutes, a couple of times a week.—*Amy*

♥ Right now, my children have very limited computer time for games: only ½ hour a week per child. They all sit and watch each other, so they're each getting 1½ hours anyway! We'll be starting typing soon, so that will be separate from game time.—*Dana*

♥ The computer and TV are only for after school. Music can be practiced whenever.—*Sharon*

♥ Computer time is limited to so many minutes per day per child, depending on age and reading capability. Those that can read earn more time because they can do research. Only part of their time is allowed for "fun." On Saturdays, none of us use the computer. I also have software installed on the computer to protect us all from uncensored junk.—*Karol*

♥ Music is essential to learning and we set aside 45 minutes for each child for music daily. The computer is for school and children get play time on the computer only on Friday at noon if all school work was done. For every hour of computer use, you have to read for two hours!—*Mitzi*

♥ My children have some colored craft sticks that they get each Monday morning. They get three 30 minute sessions on the computer and two movies a week. They turn in a stick for whatever activity they want to do and once their sticks are gone, they are finished for the week. (Our TV does not get any channels on it. We only watch clean wholesome family movies.)—*Lyn*

♥ I try to have the kids get their piano practicing in before we start school.—*Reba*

Do your children have activities such as a sports or music lessons? With so many different schedules, how do you get them to and from activities? Are you ever able to participate?

♥ We have had a few sons participate in the church softball league. It is an adult league so only ages 14 and older can play. We go as a family and watch practice and games.—*Sheri*

♥ We go to The Homeschool Hut, which offers a wide range of activities on Tuesdays and Thursdays. Because of this, each child can take at least one class. But we still narrow it down to one day a week, not both. Preparation is key!—*Lissa*

♥ It seems that many activities overlap which can be stressful. My kids are in Scouts, church events, sports, school activities, and receive party invitations. We just make it work as best we can. Sometimes, I enlist the help of other parents with carpooling. As far as having friends come over, I do try to limit that since we live in a small home. Otherwise, we just take turns. Or when one child is away at friend's house, I'll let another child have a friend over to balance things.—*Shannon*

♥ Not yet. I hope to avoid this as much as possible! We plan on handling music lessons at home, and also some sports. (Hope they like riflery, archery, and fishing!)—*Betsy*

♥ My oldest has started piano lessons and will also be doing choir this year. I drive him and either wait or run a quick errand.—*Ann*

♥ The girls are in Pioneers, which is right after school, and I participate minimally. My commitment to our adult choir is right after Pioneers, so it's a busy evening for us, but sometimes I can stay for both. This year, I volunteered to do a special presentation on baking bread, which is scheduled for early January, so I feel I'm contributing there. They also know that if someone can't bring snacks, or if there's something they need from me, they just need to ask, and I'll make it happen. My daughter had her first dance lesson yesterday; I'm investigating carpool options on that. It's close to both the church and our house, so my husband can help with driving if I'm in a pinch.—*Kate*

♥ Each of our children has had "extra-curricular" activities at some point, but generally not where they overlap and cause us to "be on the go" too much. Currently, four of them have private piano lessons where their instructor comes to our home once per week. Another has cello lessons in the local youth orchestra twice per week. Carpooling with another family has been a blessing. We have also participated in a variety of sports, music lessons, Pioneers, and 4-H.—*Janet*

♥ We have piano lessons. I go with everyone and sit and wait. We also have violin lessons. The teacher and another friend who is taking lessons both come to my house. The mom stays to visit during the lesson. We do sign-language class and I take everyone and stay and wait.—*Amy*

♥ I've tried to choose activities that more than one can participate in so that we don't have to spend so much time going back and forth. This year all the kids are playing soccer, the same day, at the same location.—*Christy*

♥ Three are taking piano lessons. One takes guitar lessons. My eldest five are taking martial arts. I drive the kids to the music lessons. Dad takes them to martial arts and participates with them. The younger ones are in Awana; older ones help in Awana at church.—*Sharon*

♥ Occasionally, we sign our children up for lessons, but not often, and it must not rule our family life. We believe in swimming lessons as a life skill and for safety, and do homeschooling swimming lessons where multiple levels are all swimming at the same time. We spent the last year on the east coast of Canada and allowed the girls to take some dance lessons as a cultural activity, but wouldn't regularly enroll them in those types of lessons. I'm sure you recognize that a mom of many could spend much of her time shuffling her children around, paying tons of money for lessons. When a child shows a definite bent towards something, we try to provide in-house instruction from a trusted friend on a short-term basis. If the interest continues and scheduling lessons doesn't infringe too much on the rest of the family, we might pursue individual training. For example, informal piano lessons came mostly from within our family, with simple instructions. As the children's skills continued, we employed a teacher. We have avoided sports because teams can be very demanding, imposing games and practice during regular family times, usually evenings and weekends. As homeschoolers, individual lessons can easily fit in during the regular public school hours, since the instructors are usually booked up after regular school lets out. We we ask for the Lord's timing, and do according to the bent of the individual child. We don't need to have our children enrolled in all the extra-curricular stuff that the relatives and neighbors think we ought to. —*Karol*

♥ We have gymnastics, ballet, and piano for our oldest three children. Also, once a week, we have homeschool co-op class. My husband drives them to co-op back and forth so I don't have to. I drive them to the other classes.—*Tina*

♥ When my children attend these types of activities, I drive and wait there. We have had emergencies come up during the classes, and I thanked God I was there!—*Mitzi*

♥ We participate in Awana, football, and voice lessons. I drive them or they carpool. I can't participate other than as a spectator right now because my younger ones need me to care for them. My husband has been able to participate in the past.—*Harriet*

♥ Yes, some. We try to limit our involvement to only what is reasonable for our family and the rest of our commitments. We typically pick a couple of activities a year and for a limited time each, such as gymnastics in the winter and baseball in the summer. We also look for activities where we can all participate—we've found a gymnastics group that is willing to run a morning winter class that allows for the participation of all the kids at the same time.—*Laurie*

♥ We have music lessons, but the teacher comes here! We also attend Awana, and everyone goes along. My husband plays softball with our church, so we all go to watch him play.—*Diana*

♥ My first daughter was in 4H and our two sons in Scouts. 4H did not work well in our area; I was driving all over the county with a van full of kids. It was nuts! Scouts was easier, but only if the boy loved it! Otherwise, it wasn't worth the effort. The kids all take piano lessons. A friend teaches and will come over to our house. We also have children's choir at church that all of them participate in.—*Reba*

♥ I am teaching piano to my girls. My daughter and I are taking violin lessons together—an instrument which I always wanted to learn, but up until now, have never had the opportunity to enjoy. —*Sarah*

♥ The oldest child drives, so he's on his own! One other has piano lessons, and Daddy takes her with her siblings taking turns, one going each week. We would like to do Sunday night or Wednesday night church activities, but it seems that someone is always too tired or grouchy to stay the whole time, or the baby's too active, so we all go home!—*Dana*

What general advice do you have for homeschooling moms with many children?

♥ Don't sweat the small stuff! Relax! If they can read, write, and do basic math, then they can teach themselves anything!—*Sheri*

♥ Combine *all* ages (yes, *all*) for subjects like history and science! It can be done! Have them all do seatwork at a table near the kitchen. You can observe and prepare meals while they work. It's also much easier to play "round robin" and look over their shoulders when they are all sitting at one general location.—*Lissa*

♥ Keep things *very* basic and only do what's important. Do as much in the home as possible, such as having music teachers come to your house. Focus on God, your husband, your family, *then* your church and homeschool.—*Karina*

♥ Hands-on activities and field trips help bring learning to life and aid in retention. Little ones can sometimes be the biggest challenge with homeschooling, so try to include them in the learning or have "special" activities for them. Try to teach more challenging subjects during the little ones' nap time.—*Janet*

♥ Keep your vision—what are your goals for your children? Have confidence. God gave these kids to you for a reason. He will equip you for the task at hand. Also, instead of struggling to teach a subject (and feeling like you're banging your head against a brick wall), just wait. Try again when the child is older. They will understand it more quickly, retain it longer, and it will be more relevant.—*Amy*

♥ If all we get done in a day is devotion and everyone eats three meals, I know I've accomplished the most important aspects of school. Sure, it's not the goal I set out for, but if I'm expecting too much, then we're all going to be miserable! With several small kids, you can't expect to have too strict of a schedule.—*Dana*

♥ Don't expect too much at first. Build up slowly. Try to have fun! Don't try to do something just because your friends are doing it. Oh, and I love Sonlight (*3)!—*Christy*

♥ Allow time for distractions. If you can get ahead at any point in the day or month, do so. Then you won't have to worry so much about catching up when "life" hits.—*Sharon*

♥ Always be aware of our tendency to live up to other people's expectations, rather than the Lord's. We are not to be man-pleasers, but God-pleasers. Jesus came to give us life more abundantly, and he whom the Son sets free is free indeed. If your educational system doesn't bring life, then I'd question whether it is of God. He puts before us life and death, blessings and curses. Choose life!—*Karol*

♥ Plan, prepare in advance, and pray for wisdom.—*Tina*

♥ Take a time for rest every day! If Mama's day does not start with prayer, you are going to pray that it did!—*Mitzi*

♥ Everything will come together in its own time. Don't rush your children. Let them learn at their own pace. And don't compare them to public school children or a public school education.—*Lyn*

♥ Enjoy your children! They grow up so fast! Have the older ones help the younger ones as much as possible.—*Harriet*

♥ Train the young ones in obedience and help them learn to sit and play quietly for short periods of time. When I need to work with the older ones, I put out a large blanket and a basket full of books for the small children. Now they know what this means, and they come right over, sit down and start choosing books to look at. They are capable of doing something like this (with patience and practice) for 15 minutes at a time. Children need to be trained in self-discipline and faithfulness with a task so that you can count on them to complete some tasks independently. Also, find school materials or curricula that are designed to include multiple ages so that you don't need separate materials for everyone for every subject!—*Laurie*

♥ Get the oldest ones to read as soon as possible. Before long, they can work fairly independently. Don't burn yourself and your kids out! Stay away from homeschooling magazines with the gushing stories of wonderful perfect homeschoolers who spin wool, sew their own clothes, bake all their own bread, send kids to Harvard, and never utter a sinful word. No one needs to live with pressure like that! I recommend *The Lost Tools of Learning* (*4) by Dorothy Sayers, *Recovering the Lost Tools of Learning* (*5) by Douglas Wilson and *The Well-Trained Mind* (*6) by Susan Wise Bauer and Jessie Wise. These books helped me define a philosophy and a structure.—*Reba*

Chapter Six

The "Wife" Part of Being a Mother

"The heart of her husband safely trusts her;
So he will have no lack of gain.
She does him good and not evil
All the days of her life. ...
Her husband praises her also:
'Many women do noble things,
but you surpass them all.'"
Proverbs 31:11–12,28–29

A mother who is busy nursing, potty-training, cooking, and teaching can easily forget her first calling as a wife. Yet, the closer the bond of a husband and wife, the closer the bond of the whole family. In this chapter, mothers of many share their thoughts about meeting the needs of their husbands, and the joy it brings to their families.

Children (and a gushing wife!) are so excited to see Dad when he comes home from work! What are your tips for not overwhelming him?

♥ My husband is home most of the time but when he does come home from driving or going to town, there honestly isn't much fan fair!—*Sheri*

♥ We try to have the house clean, greet him with smiles and have dinner on the table when he walks in. As long as the food's on the table, everything's good.—*Lissa*

♥ Gushing wife?! How about climbing-the-walls-wife? I know you're not supposed to overwhelm him—but we do it anyways! My husband expects it now and likes the attention. He can have his quiet time later. Why dash the excitement of having Daddy come home?—*Shannon*

♥ Don't hit him with all your woes before he even gets the door closed! I try to let him get in, unload his bag, and take off his coat before letting the kids loose, but exuberance usually wins. He doesn't seem to mind, though!—*Ann*

♥ I let my husband come to me in the kitchen, instead of waiting for him at the door. Usually, the kids rush to him when he comes in the door. By the time he shakes them off and makes it to the kitchen, he's really wanting a hug and kiss from me. I try to turn away from whatever I'm doing and give him a minute of attention. Then, he usually goes to our room to change out of his work clothes and we give him a few minutes of time alone. He doesn't seem to be overly sensitive about being crowded when he gets home, but on the rare occasions when he really needs space, he just expresses that to the kids. They know we'll all be eating dinner together soon.—*Kate*

♥ I try to let him at least get out of the car!—*Diana*

♥ We all try to greet dad first and ask about *his* day, before our own sharing or business matters that are pressing.—*Laurie*

♥ We try to clean the first room he comes into and have something cooking when he gets home. Bake an onion, if necessary.—*Mitzi*

♥ My dear husband works from home three times a week, so this isn't an issue. He doesn't get overwhelmed. He loves it when they meet him at the door all excited and jumping on him!—*Tina*

♥ We have found that most of this is my husband's responsibility. He needs to be prepared to receive all the hugs and chatter. At times while driving home, he has had to pray earnestly that he would graciously receive all the children's love. The best part of my day is when I see my husband's car drive down our street. I always try to greet him with a (hot) kiss and hug, then if the children are upon him, I drop into the peripheral. We try to avoid high demands on Daddy (fix this and that!) when he first arrives home.—*Karol*

♥ He's as thrilled to see the kids as they are to see him! He loves that they run to see him!—*Sharon*

♥ Lately, he'd probably be happy if I did "overwhelm" him! We've just asked the kids to not bombard him with questions, but otherwise, he's happy to hear about our day.—*Dana*

♥ I told my kids that Daddy couldn't enjoy us if we were fighting to get to the door first and shouting the loudest to get his attention. Have them each pick one thing from the day to tell him. Assign who goes first. After they tell him one thing, have them be quiet and train them to listen to how *his* day was.—*Amy*

♥ Have a home that is a sanctuary and retreat for him. Create an atmosphere that showers him with love. Try not to attack with the problems of the day as soon as he walks in, but instead, show excitement. My husband loves it when the kids are eager to see him.—*Janet*

Do you have time alone with your husband every day without the children interrupting?

♥ Yes. We get to talk after the kids are in bed after 8 p.m. We also talk about our day when the kids are cleaning up dinner. Alone time is essential with your husband every day! Shut a door if necessary and make it as sacred as Bible time. You were a wife before you had children!—*Lissa*

♥ Yes, we talk each day about our lives. Sometimes, a lot of times, we are interrupted several times. We shoo the kids away and tell them it's Mommy/Daddy time. Sometimes they're good with this, and other times they're impatient. We work around it.—*Shannon*

♥ Well, we sleep together! If he doesn't fall asleep, we talk. If I can manage to get awake in the mornings, we talk. Other than that, we steal moments away together, like if he needs to do a quick drive to get supplies for his shop, I'll tag along.—*Karina*

♥ No bedtime is too early! Get those kids down *as soon as possible*! This is not a joke!—*Betsy*

♥ After the kids are in bed is usually our time. Right now, we have a baby in our bed most of the night, so we are never quite completely alone.—*Ann*

♥ We don't always have alone time, but we've both learned how to get by with less. Sometimes, we can watch TV together on an evening when my husband doesn't have meetings, or read in bed together. If we need time to discuss something away from the kids' ears, we simply tell them that Mom and Dad need to talk. They need to find something to do and make themselves scarce.—*Kate*

♥ Yes, in the evenings after the children are in bed. We also do quite a bit of traveling and love to spend those hours on the road talking together, while the children do their own activities in the back seats.—*Sarah*

♥ No, I don't except when we are asleep.—*Diana*

♥ Occasionally, we take a 15 minute walk. That's about it.—*Reba*

♥ We usually spend time together in the morning after the kids have gone to school. We still have one child with us. If we go for a walk, she comes with us and it seems to work out. It is hard to find time alone.—*Betty*

♥ All of the kids, even the 13-year-old is in bed by 9 p.m. We have until around 10 p.m. to be alone.—*Mery*

♥ We often try to debrief for a few minutes after he first gets home. We have tried to help the children learn to be patient and let Mom and Dad have that time first, and then they get Dad time, too! We also generally spend some time together after the children go to bed at night, but this may change as the children get older and stay up later.—*Laurie*

♥ We usually shower together before bed. This is when we talk about our day...mostly!—*Harriet*

♥ We have the opportunity to be alone every day after the children go to bed. I also occasionally go out for lunch with him and leave the children at home.—*Lyn*

♥ My husband presently works from home. We share morning coffee time together, although not always alone. We usually connect alone before bedtime after the little people are bedded down. We read a Bible-based book aloud to each other around the house, in bed, or while driving. My husband doesn't do well with our quiet-time if the children are noisy around us. Sometimes, we'll put a video in for them if we really need time to talk, or we'll get a babysitter while we go out to a coffee shop to talk privately.—*Karol*

♥ We're alone only after the kids are in bed, normally. But we do go out, even to the store, just the two of us, once every couple weeks, since our eldest is old enough to watch the others for a while.— *Sharon*

♥ No, not everyday. We aim for "couch time" where we just sit and talk and instruct the kids not to interrupt. When we do this, our youngest two love it. You can tell it makes them feel really secure. —*Christy*

♥ No, that's not happening. We probably could have quiet time after the kids go to bed. Or, we could in the morning, as they've been sleeping in.—*Dana*

♥ After the kids are in bed. Sometimes, if we need to we'll go sit on the porch for a private conversation. We will make sure everyone has a job or activity to do and then take the baby with us.—*Amy*

♥ We try to get some time together after dinner. Other times, we will feed the children dinner and then after they are ready for bed, we will have an "at home date night"—a movie for the kids while we enjoy a nice quiet dinner together.—*Janet*

How often do you go on dates?

♥ Once a week...always! On Saturday mornings, we go out for breakfast. (I am a cheap date, what can I say!)—*Lissa*

♥ Nothing is scheduled, but there are always weddings, and other dinner events—especially in the Marine Corps.—*Shannon*

♥ Not very often. We're on a budget and live far from family, so babysitting is generally difficult to swing. I would estimate we go out alone or with only an infant six or eight times per year.—*Betsy*

♥ Dates? What are those? I think we only went out by ourselves once this past year! We would like to do it more often, but time and money don't allow for much.—*Ann*

♥ I would guess that we average a "date" every six months. It's funny, because this was more important to me when we were first married. It was so quiet being at home with one baby. However, my husband was happiest at home with us, and didn't have that need to get out like I did. I think my needs have changed in the meantime. I'm happier to have a "date" at home, because the effort that it takes us to "get out" is not worth it. Two weeks ago, we bought a ribeye steak to grill after the kids were in bed, shared a little wine and rented a movie. I thought it was more fun than spending $20 on a sitter, $20 on movie tickets, and getting home late and tired.—*Kate*

♥ Not regularly. Because we spend so much time alone every evening, we don't feel like we're actually suffering from a lack of dates.—*Sarah*

♥ Our birthdays and anniversary.—*Reba*

♥ We aim for once a month. We have an extra adult living with us and have had someone like this for a few years now. It is definitely a mutually beneficial situation. We are able to provide a family environment and free room and board for her. She helps me with cleaning and dishes and allows us to get out for an occasional date! Praise God for this blessing! I encourage all young moms to pray for such an arrangement. We love it!—*Laurie*

♥ Once a week. We've been doing this since our second child was born. We couldn't afford much in the beginning so we hired a homeschooled teenager, packed dinner, and went for a walk. We recently bought two beach cruisers and go on bike rides for our dates.—*Tina*

♥ Not often enough! I think a "formal" date should be once a month. Since both sets of grandparents live within 15 minutes, it would be nice to have a break once a week, but I'm dreaming again!—*Dana*

♥ Every day. We just take our kids with us. Really, we try to not focus on "I must get away." Well-trained children are not something to be escaped, but enjoyed. Every so often, my husband and I will order Chinese food to eat after the kids go to bed, though.—*Amy*

♥ Dates are an important part of our relationship, however not always feasible or available with a large family and little outside help. Swapping with a friend to have a "feed and ready for bed" date night has worked for us in the past. A friend and I would swap. This is how it worked: the family would have the children fed and in pajamas. The babysitting mom would arrive and spend time reading or overseeing a quiet activity, then put the children in bed. The date may be a little later, but it allowed the husband and wife time away together. Then in a couple of weeks the same would be reciprocated for the babysitting mom.—*Janet*

♥ Until our eldest daughters were of babysitting age (and we had a cell phone), we didn't do any regular dates. Now, we try to have a date once a week, but it isn't necessarily romantic; sometimes, we get errands done. Now that our eldest are 21 and 20, we can even get away with Baby for a night at a hotel. It was a long wait, but worth it for these great times!—*Karol*

Do you ever get away for a few days? How do you arrange for this?

♥ Yes, when grandparents can watch the kids. We've also hired friends' daughters for a couple of nights. It's about once a year or so.—*Lissa*

♥ Not really, unless it's an event. My parents or my in-laws will watch them. We divide them up if necessary.—*Shannon*

♥ It depends on where things are at with the baby. We have adult children so they can take over. Our 25th anniversary is coming up next year, so hopefully?—*Karina*

♥ We did once through a happenstance set of circumstances that will never happen again. We had only two kids then and they stayed with a grandma. We're planning a trip for 30 years from now to give ourselves something to think about.—*Betsy*

♥ We were able to take a 3 1/2 week trip to Europe last summer, mostly graduate school related for my husband, but we added a few extra days after his class was done and toured Germany by ourselves. My sister watched the kids for us.—*Ann*

♥ We went to Hawaii for five days once. Friends took the children and it worked out great. This coming summer, a friend is taking our three oldest, and we (and baby) are going to California for a weekend. My husband has business there, but we'll be there for my birthday. We're both excited for the alone time. It's been a while!—*Kate*

♥ About once a year, we've gone out for a night or two. The children stayed with their grandparents. This has been so amazing. The last time we went, our baby was still too young to be away from us for the weekend so he came along, but it didn't detract from our time together at all. We're fortunate to have my husband's parents living close by who are willing to babysit.—*Sarah*

♥ If we go away, we usually always take the kids. I don't feel I need days away from them. Just a couple of hours is enough.—*Mery*

♥ We do an annual homeschool conference as a weekend away.—*Diana*

♥ Not for several days at a time. However, we do occasionally get away for an overnight date. We usually manage this about every couple years or so, when the "baby" is 1½ or 2 and old enough to stay the night with a grandparent or aunt.—*Laurie*

♥ Yes. Ask friends or parents to watch the children. We just went for a few days together and I had the kids in pairs at different houses. I am very blessed in that my parents will also take all six of them. —*Harriet*

♥ About once or twice a year for birthdays or anniversaries. Either his mom or my mom will come to our house since it's baby-proofed. It's a lot of fun. If we have a baby, then we will stay local or take him/her overnight. We have done it a lot of different ways. —*Tina*

♥ We've had grandmas come, and once we had an aunty and a teen cousin come. The dear children love it, and it lets the grandmas be grandmas just the way they like it, without Mama looking over their shoulders, pooh-poohing all the sugar they are doling out.—*Karol*

♥ For anniversaries, the grandparents are happy to divide the kids and help out.—*Christy*

♥ We were given tickets to a marriage retreat last fall. We scrounged up the money for a hotel and each set of grandparents had the kids for one day. Otherwise, I'd rather the grandparents take the kids and us just stay home together! We get time off when we're in the hospital with a new baby, if that counts!—*Dana*

♥ Every year, we go to the homeschool convention in our area. My parents watch the kids for two and a half days and two nights.—*Amy*

♥ Only twice in our 19 years of marriage have we "gotten away" for a weekend each time. One time the children's grandmother came over and another time a couple from church watched them and blessed us with that special time.—*Janet*

How does your big family cope with changes when your husband is not able to participate in family life as normal?

♥ My husband is in the military so I have a lot of experience with being a "single" mom. He even deployed to Iraq for a year in 2004–2005. It was challenging, and we made adjustments. As a single mom, you just have to remain in control and be firm. I'll admit, I found that leaves less room for nurturing and the softer side of being a mommy. Kids need the balance of a mother and father and family life is definitely disrupted when one parent is missing.—*Shannon*

♥ Make the times count when you are together. Children know when parents have a good relationship, whether they are both physically there each day or not. Mothers can always refer to Daddy, and his desires and wishes, even if he isn't right there.—*Karina*

♥ We get very sad. If possible, I try to have a field trip or invite a friend to visit us and break up our long lonely days without him.—*Betsy*

♥ Usually, it is just me who gets cranky, especially at bedtime—my least favorite time! We have experienced this a few times and have come through it okay. We talk about Daddy not being there ahead of time so that they know, but we still have to go over it again and again.—*Ann*

♥ Our daily traditions—mealtimes together, prayer, activities together—help. The fact that we're getting things done together also helps pass the time. We also developed traditions to have when my husband is away; one is special stories that I only tell the girls on Tuesday nights when he's at meetings. Another is "breakfast for dinner" if he's away on a trip. While he's gone, we plan special things for when he comes home, like a meal, sign, or gift they've made. We pray for his safety together and call him if there's the opportunity.—*Kate*

♥ Dad's absence truly is a challenge, and one in which the Lord continues to work on me. Any illness or traveling has its set of challenges and does alter the "routine" of things. Praise the Lord that He is faithful and never leaves us.—*Janet*

♥ My dear husband was just traveling for four days. Granted, it's not too long of a time, but it was a great bonding time for the kids and me. We could do messy things all day long and not have to worry about dinner prep. (We ate *very* simply.) I found that I made more of an effort to plan fun outings with the kids, knowing I was the only parent. We did all sorts of cool things. And then we really appreciated him when he got home.—*Amy*

♥ You cannot be "father" to the children anything like your dear husband can. Just recognize that fact. Trust that *the* Father will fill in *all* the gaps we have.—*Karol*

♥ We try our best to rearrange our schedules to accommodate Dad's schedule. Over time, we can adjust our "normal" to fit the needs of our family and Dad's schedule. When he is home on a day off, we take time to eat meals together and spend time together. When he is working later, I try to feed the kids before he gets home, so that they are ready to start the bedtime routine with him when he gets here. This allows a relaxed, regular bedtime routine rather than a rushed meal and hurried bedtime. If Dad is going to be gone, we just adjust our plans. I don't even *try* to function the same if I know I'm on my own for a day or two. I know that I'm not going to have the energy to do it all. We just pull back a bit and find something fun to do together, like plan a meal that Dad doesn't like while he's not here to be tortured by it!—*Laurie*

♥ We talk a lot on the phone with him. We pray *a lot* more together throughout the hard times when Daddy is gone. It is a challenge. We are a military family and my husband leaves often. However, we have been so blessed that it hasn't been for as long as a year, like many other soldiers. Also, there are times that I really rely on the Body of Christ to come alongside and help me. They are always there and bless us, helping with laundry or cleaning.—*Diana*

♥ Daddy's schedule and routine dictate our family's activities. He is home very little and travels quite a bit, as well. I tend to operate pretty independently. My husband is an academic and theologian. If it has to do with home maintenance, food, car, the home, or family, that's my area. There are frustrations with that arrangement, but mostly it works, because it has to. When he is teaching in another country for weeks at a time, life gets a little stressful, but mostly, it's business as usual. What is difficult is when *Mom* is out of commission! Our last baby was a surprise C-Section, followed by a four week nasty infection. We have friends who took the kids for a few days and provided meals. What a blessing! My husband nearly lost his mind though! (And the house was a crazy mess!)—*Reba*

♥ When we had two or three children, I used to invite them all into our master bed to sleep when Daddy was gone to keep me company. Now, they're too big to all fit, so I pull their mattress into our bedroom and we still have our sleepover when Daddy's gone. Sometimes we've had one last sleepover when Daddy gets back to have family bonding time.—*Sarah*

At the end of the day, how do you avoid exhaustion? Do you ever feel "touched out" from meeting the needs of the children, when your husband needs you as well?

♥ I think that since I have the kids helping me out all day that I am less exhausted than I was when I only had toddlers/babies. It's just a season of life that will pass quickly. You'll forget about it all too fast! Coffee also is a good start to an evening together!—*Lissa*

♥ I'm not the only one? I thought I was weird! My husband teases sometimes and tells the kids to stop touching me so much! We usually have a drink and watch TV or read to relax. We'll discuss the news or a show. We will make time for intimacy, as well.—*Shannon*

♥ I'm a night person and my husband isn't, so he'll tend to fall asleep when his head hits the pillow. It is a fine balance to keep him and the children satisfied, but he always comes first.—*Karina*

♥ My time with my husband is the best thing that happens to me in a day. He's usually just as tired as I am so we're happy to collapse on the couch together. I get very tired of being climbed on by kids all day (usually by about 8 a.m.), but for me this doesn't translate into any need to avoid him. —*Betsy*

♥ I guess if I'm really tired out, I try to have a nap in the early afternoon. That way I can better handle everything later in the day. However, this usually only happens if I'm pregnant and literally can't keep my eyes open. I guess my best answer would be that I try to pace myself during the day and stay in a good frame of mind. Also, going to bed earlier (9 p.m.) is so much better. Instead of stressing about getting right to sleep, there is more time to relax, unwind, and catch up with each other on the day. —*Kimi*

♥ Sometimes, especially when there is a tiny baby in the house, I do feel very "touched out." Being able to express my feelings of suffocation help my husband understand why I'm "touched out." Constant communication between the two of us has helped with the emotional aspect of this. I need to be a wife, too, so it's important for us to be creative sometimes, and find a way for the husband/wife relationship to regain priority. —*Kate*

♥ I enjoy a lot of touch! However, the challenge for me is that as soon as I hit the pillow, I'm asleep! So, we've found that if my husband and I want to talk, then we sit up on the couch in the living room together after the little ones are asleep. Our children start going to bed at 7 p.m. and are quiet by 8 p.m. This leaves us to have the evening alone. We've found we have to go to bed a bit earlier when we want to meet each other's touch needs before I crash. —*Sarah*

♥ He is usually the one with too much to do! Yes, I often feel touched out, empty, used up! I guess that's a good topic of conversation with husbands: a simple backrub, DQ treat, a handful of daisies. It doesn't take much to "refloat" gal's boat sometimes! A little nurturing for the family nurturer? —*Reba*

♥ I am not the best at this. Often, we are both so tired we just lay in bed and watch a movie together. Does that count? I really try to submit to his physical needs and realize that God gave him desires and be thankful that it is me he desires! —*Diana*

♥ It helps tremendously when I am faithful to go to bed on time, get enough sleep, and get an early start in the morning. It seems we are most effective and efficient in the mornings—so when we get a good, early start, we accomplish more for the day and can have a more relaxed afternoon and evening. And, of course, I often feel "touched out" given that I am always touched constantly all day long! But, I've also come to see the legitimacy and importance of my husband's needs. Just as I trust him to be sensitive to my needs and to put my needs above his, I also need to be sensitive to his needs and consider him more important than myself. This is not an easy thing to live out daily, but a life-changing and marriage-saving Biblical principle when it is implemented in our lives!—*Laurie*

♥ I try to maintain a one-hour quiet-time in the afternoons. This has been mandatory as long as I've had kids. It helps me keep my sanity and store up energy for the evening.—*Harriet*

♥ I don't really ever feel exhausted. If I do, I go to bed with the kids at 9 p.m. You have to take care of yourself and listen to your body. My dear husband does the same if he's tired. Again, it's not a science. You don't have to spend "1 hour of quality time" with your husband everyday to have a good marriage. You need to try, but don't feel guilty if you are too tired and need rest! Love each other —that's what is important. Even if you can take a shower together or just talk in bed for a few minutes, that can be more fulfilling and worthwhile than a "planned amount of time." Again, what would God want for Himself? A half hour everyday or any moment thinking and praying and reading scripture sprinkled throughout the day? I like both ideas, but don't make the time allotment what it's all about—make it about the relationship and loving each other.—*Tina*

♥ Certain times in family life, I am absolutely feeling "pawed" and don't even want a hint of what my dear husband wants. It's been a difficult area to transcend in many ways, and I haven't dealt with it well for many years. My husband didn't handle it well either. But we are on "the other side" now, and feeling in many ways that our exciting love-life is coming back. My mindset was definitely flawed from my upbringing. I'd say the very biggest thing to work on is communication about each others' needs and desires. Work at *not* being exhausted. Change the way your family/home functions. If your husband wants personal attention and a good sex-life, then he might have some adjustments to make himself. You might suggest he help out more, lower his standards, or pay for a babysitter. Almost any man would take a simpler meal or a dirty floor to have a passionate wife!—*Karol*

♥ I am normally completely spent and exhausted by the end of the day. Occasionally, I'll have my husband help with more things around the house, and then feel more like spending quality time with him.—*Sharon*

♥ This is hard, isn't it? When my children were younger and I was new at being a mom, I definitely remember feeling "touched out." But I have gotten over it—or used to it. Even if we are both exhausted, we try hard to give short updates from our day.—*Christy*

♥ He's usually the one who falls asleep before I get done brushing my teeth! We just aren't doing well with this; I guess I need the suggestions from the other ladies! Feeling "touched out" is exactly how I would describe it. He wants to hug me in the kitchen while I'm making dinner and still in Mom-mode. My daughter, age 10, has started needing more touch lately, and sometimes I almost cringe; I'm hoping she doesn't notice any cringing!—*Dana*

♥ Make sure to leave something of yourself for him. Long after the kids are gone, he'll still be there. The Lord will fill you up where you are lacking. I know He does for me!—*Amy*

♥ I believe most moms have that feeling—especially after caring for little ones all day. But, it is important to keep contact with our husbands throughout the day through loving affection.—*Janet*

Looking back on the earlier part of your marriage and child-rearing, are there changes you could have made then that would have made now easier?

♥ Oh, yes! We should have realized that we were doing too much with our church and missing out on some of the best parts of being parents. Fortunately, we realized the mistakes we were making early in our marriage and made a conscious effort to change them. Now, we regularly re-evaluate the demands the church is making on our family and home, my emotional/physical health, and how we are doing as parents and as spouses. I wish we had read *Love and Respect*(*1) earlier. We're planning to lead a couples' Bible

study on the book together because we think it's so important.—
Kimi

♥ I'd like to share how important I think the mother's health—
physical, spiritual, emotional, and mental—is to everyone in the
home. Mother sets the tone for everyone else in the house, yet so
many moms put their health last. One can't expect a woman who's
drained, exhausted, and stressed to create an environment that's
warm, nurturing, and safe. We make the most mistakes when
we're tired—whether we're driving or caring for kids. That is why
it has been so important for me to regain physical health between
pregnancies. It takes patience and a lot of work. Other things that
I do for my own physical health include journaling, taking
excellent vitamins, seeing the chiropractor if my back is painful,
eating healthfully, working out, and getting enough sleep. I also do
a juice fast/detox after completing nursing each child. My
husband and I both know from experience that our household
runs best when I'm in good shape. Health is a priority! My contact
with friends, family, and my spouse help fill the emotional need to
be understood by other adults. When I need support, I take action.
If I need a listening ear, I call my sister. I try to be proactive.

Another huge factor in our ability to maintain a large family is
God's blessing of discipline. I truly believe that if we had not been
able to establish effective discipline for our first child, I would not
be equipped to care for many more children. My husband I both
had to invent our own routine for showing our oldest boundaries
in a firm yet loving way. We are told so many times how "lucky"
we are that we got "good kids" by people who obviously think it's
up to chance whether you have a child that behaves. I always smile
and think to myself, "You're giving luck too much credit, and
you're giving me too little!" It should be no surprise that following
God's commands to discipline our children, and bring them up in
the nurture and admonition of the Lord, will yield good fruit. Yet,
we continually pray that God will show us how to be better parents
to all of our children.—*Kate*

♥ We thank the Lord for opening our eyes and showing us in His
Word all that we need to know. From a practical sense, it would
have been better to train our children earlier and not have catered
to our eldest in the realms of sleeping, eating, likes and dislikes.
We could have served him better with discipline, but have learned

and applied those teachings to our subsequent children, and with him as we gained wisdom.—*Janet*

♥ I wish I would have learned to honor my husband and submit to his authority earlier. My lack of respect caused a great deal of friction in the early years of our marriage. God has blessed me with an amazing husband and I would do well to follow his lead. Even in the areas I might feel he's lacking, God's commandment to honor and obey still stand. I recommend the following books to aid your family: *To Train Up a Child* (*2) by Michael and Debi Pearl, *Educating the Whole-Hearted Child* (*3) by Clay Clarkson, and *Raising Godly Tomatoes* (*4) by L. Elizabeth Krueger.—*Amy*

♥ I wish I would have understood what a Godly wife was. I also wish I had understood about serving and hard work. We didn't teach these to our oldest because we just didn't know. I also wish I would have had more fun; I had so many unrealistic expectations! —*Dana*

♥ I'd have started with a front-loading washing machine and a king-size bed! I'd have started with co-sleeping instead of a crib. I'd eat more raw food, which eliminates the need for some of the regular kitchen gadgets. I'd rather have two fridges and no stove. It's much harder to change all my children's taste buds now that they are developed for unhealthy foods. I'd forget what everybody else thinks my family ought to do/be/look like, and have a heart only to please God. That's all that matters. A few weeks after my sister's house burned down on the Atlantic coast, we put our own house on the market, gave most of our possessions away, and my dear husband and I (with our seven youngest children) piled in a station wagon and a van with as much stuff as we could cram in, and drove across the continent to build a better relationship with my sister. Truly, what freedom we felt! It's been an absolutely awesome experience and adventure, and it continues to get better and better.

Now, we've decided to head south for the winter, to glean from a ministry. We don't know what to exactly expect, but we know that without faith it is *impossible* to please God. We are so excited, and learning much from our own children. Unless we become like these little ones, who trust their papa for absolutely every good thing, then we can not enter into the Kingdom of God. I am determined to walk in faith rather than fear. We have no place lined up for housing when we get there. But should we be worried?

No. Two years ago, we would have thought this irresponsible, scary, and ridiculous with so many children dependent on us. But today, we have a stronger faith in the goodness of the Lord and have said "no" to fear. We walk by faith and not by sight.—*Karol*

♥ I should have spent more time being husband-centered and focused on him, rather than primarily learning to be a good mother. I also would have finished my education. Now, there isn't time.—*Diana*

♥ It seems like the younger ones took up so much of my time! I wish now that I would have spent more time talking to and encouraging the older ones that were in school. Things may have gone a little smoother for them.—*Betty*

♥ Before marriage, we should have had financial counseling! We aren't able to be on the same page and that is *hard*. I wish we talked and planned more. It's just not my husband's approach to life, so I think up "plans" but roll with the punches.—*Reba*

♥ I would have loved if I had been able to read *Created to be His Helpmeet* (*5) by Debi Pearl before I was married. 15 years later, I know how to be a better wife! You have to read this book if you haven't yet!—*Tina*

♥ I wish I would've relaxed more and held my oldest more when she asked me to. I wish I would've ditched perfectionism earlier—I am still working on it! I wish I would've said yes to more things that were really inconsequential. Take a deep breath, stay present in the moment, learn what love really looks like. Praise God in the midst of your challenges because He's working something really good in the midst of them. My relational disconnects and unloving behaviors towards my children are my #1 wish-I-would've-done-that-differently: not the curriculum, not the chore charts, not the meal plans or the organized days or the field trips or the frequency of the Bible study lessons. I'm so thankful to have a God who redeems and restores that which has been broken and harmed through my ignorance and mistakes. May you grow in ever increasing awareness of how great the Father loves you and how much grace there is for every season of life.—*Harriet*

Chapter Seven

Spiritual Wisdom

"She opens her mouth with wisdom,
And on her tongue is the law of kindness."
Proverbs 31:26

Besides our husbands, our children are our greatest earthly treasures. But we want them to be heavenly treasures, too. How can we give our all to train up these children in the way they should go, and guide them toward the ultimate goal of eternal life with our Savior? These mothers describe God's grace in allowing them to be instruments of His hands, keeping His little lambs in the one true faith.

When do you find time to have family or personal devotions?

♥ We have time in the evening with Daddy! We call it family worship! The kids choose a few songs to sing. We listen to a passage from the Bible and my husband asks them what they think it means and corrects their thoughts as we go along. It really sticks with them, too! We also have "quiz time" on Sunday nights where my husband sees how much they can remember of what the pastor said in church that morning. They tell what they remember and they earn a special dessert if they impress Daddy enough.—*Lissa*

♥ 7 a.m. each morning, with whomever is awake.—*Karina*

♥ Just as my own father did, my husband reads from the Scriptures at the end of each breakfast. Right now, we're reading the book of Psalms. No matter how hectic the day is, we're all starting out together at breakfast, so it's the best time for us to have regular devotions.—*Kate*

♥ I do "school time" devotions with the kids in the morning, and Daddy usually does prayers at bedtime. Sometimes we get a "teachable moment" and have a spontaneous discussion.—*Dana*

♥ Again, this is done by living our life. We don't actually do a particular "devotional" program nor schedule a specific time.—*Karol*

♥ We try to have devotions regularly after dinner. That is the best time for us since we are all home and it's a routine.—*Tina*

♥ I try to read the Bible with the children after breakfast but I'm not always as consistent as I would like to be.—*Sheri*

♥ Usually we do this in the mornings, but we've been forgetting recently. The Enemy has been working overtime to make these past four weeks tight and over-scheduled in the early mornings.—*Mitzi*

♥ We read the Bible together first thing every morning before breakfast and also at night before bed.—*Lyn*

♥ We have a brief devotional time during our schooling each day. We also try to do a family worship time a couple of times a week after breakfast. We pray, sing, and study the Word together. This home worship time really helps children become accustomed to corporate worship settings and church functions in general.—*Laurie*

♥ Devotion time is in the morning. My husband and I get up first and have our own quiet prayer time. Then, the children get up and we all sit together while my husband reads some Scripture.—*Sarah*

♥ Family devotions are done whenever we can fit them into the schedule. I normally can incorporate them into the Bible lessons. —*Sharon*

♥ Time for personal devotion and prayer is a problem for me, and I suspect I'm not alone. Like hygiene, the best case scenario is getting up early to get it done. But one kid is an early riser, and I'm usually not too inclined to roll out of bed before he does. If the toddler and baby nap at the same time, I can sneak away for devotion, but I also hate to give up the alone time with the older kid, and there's no shortage of other work tempting me away from it either. Postpartum is absolutely terrible—I'm so exhausted that if I do get a minute alone I just fall asleep. I highly recommend private confession with a minister for all people. This is the only time I can count on to be completely uninterrupted.—*Betsy*

♥ I do devotions with the kids every morning. My husband does them every night.—*Amy*

What types of devotions appeal to your family which spans several age and interest levels?

♥ I read a chapter from the Bible and we talk about it. Then, one child gets to draw a picture of the subject on a 5x7 card. The cards are kept for review every once in a while. I still have the cards that the older children drew when they were little; they are one of my prized possessions.—*Sheri*

♥ The Bible is and should be interesting to all age groups. Every age can tell something about what was just read. Devotion books can be nice, but they can sometimes either distract from the Word of God, or the family can become so overwhelmed with the activities required that they end up quitting it altogether. Reading a verse or two from the Bible *is* interesting if read with enthusiasm! It's not about entertainment, but about content. Every age can understand the Bible! We didn't always see it this way, but *wow*, have we seen a difference since we changed routes. We also do a short catechism with the kids on a regular basis.—*Lissa*

♥ We have a wide variety since we "blend" denominations. My kids go to Catholic religious education classes, Sunday School, and AWANA. We read children's devotions at home and say prayers at mealtime and bedtime. We're far from perfect, but we do try to teach our children about God's love and grace.—*Shannon*

♥ Lately, we have been learning the commandments and their meanings from the Luther's *Small Catechism* (*1). Everyone is eager to have their turn to recite. We discuss the sermon on Sundays and go over the readings and Sunday School lesson.—*Ann*

♥ I find that children are especially interested in the Psalms and Bible stories. They frequently ask questions. Also, we spend a week on each Psalm, rereading it each day, which has helped them memorize portions of them, too. We have devotion books and Bible Story books that we share with the kids when we have reading time before bed, but that isn't a regular thing.—*Kate*

♥ We have done both catechisms and the reading of scripture in small segments with applicable discussion. More in-depth, age-appropriate studies are done first thing in the morning, with my husband teaching the older boys using book studies. The younger children and I often study Proverbs and good character books with key Scripture themes.—*Janet*

♥ We read the Bible. It's the best devotion out there. Occasionally, we'll use Luther's *Catechism.*—*Amy*

♥ We're doing Clarkson's *Our 24 Family Ways* (*2) and really enjoy it. They don't make it too simple; I think it meets each child where he or she is at. I'm amazed at how kids can really get deep ideas!—*Dana*

♥ In addition to our Christian homeschool curriculum, when we're in the car, I only have on Christian music.—*Sharon*

♥ We talk about the Lord throughout our day. We recite Scripture as it pertains to our situation. We share what the Lord has told us with whomever is around at the moment. We have constant conversations about the goodness of the Lord, about what the cross provided for us. Most evenings we share communion, which also includes checking our hearts for forgiveness. We read aloud Christian books and biographies, read and share testimonies we find online, and listen to Christian music throughout the day. I don't believe that Christ sat down at a particular time each day with His disciples to have devotions. He taught as they walked and lived their lives. I personally feel that Christians have unfortunately compartmentalized all areas of our lives, but Christ has called us to one whole life.—*Karol*

♥ We do a traditional reading of scripture using a children's Bible with pictures. All children have a copy of the Bible. The children can either follow along while Daddy reads or draw a picture of the story. They are all working on creating their own Bibles. We are done with the Old Testament, and half way done with New Testament. It has taken us 2 years so far to complete it. We sometimes have the older children read and teach. Coloring for the younger children helps focus attention. I usually have the older children write a paragraph summary of the story.—*Tina*

♥ We listen to the Bible on tape. We have a reading plan that has us reading through the entire Bible in 90 days. Once we finish the Bible, we start over again. Plus, they get little "life lessons" through out the day.—*Lyn*

♥ We sing praise and worship songs together, work through a devotion book, spend time praying for one another, and Scripture reading time. I don't try to find something of interest for everyone. Rather, I try to discern what is relevant for our family as a whole. —*Harriet*

♥ We primarily use the Bible as our devotional. My husband usually organizes this time and leads it. We will often repeat a worship song or hymn for many family worship times in a row to help the children become familiar with it before we change to something different. He usually reads a short passage from the Scriptures, often from the section of Scripture we are currently studying at church.—*Laurie*

♥ Attend Dr. Bender's Concordia Catechetical Academy (*3) next June! You can download and print Dr. Bender's Congregation at Prayer each week for daily catechesis. It is set up for daily family devotions/catechesis with scripture reading, hymns, and praying the catechism. You can shorten it as needed to fit your family. It's how we begin our school day and end our family evening meals. Sometimes, we do an abbreviated version, but the children absorb it quickly and there's no need for kiddie devotions.—*Reba*

Do all of the children participate in these devotions? Do you allow the younger ones to eat or play during devotion?

♥ We are all at the table after breakfast. They all participate in the conversation after the reading or I will ask them questions if they don't offer any input.—*Sheri*

♥ Yes, we all participate and listen! Children 2 and older must sit still, as this is learning to respect God and His Word. It is also training for sitting in church. Children can also color something about the Scriptures being read. Of course, babies just sit and play.

On Mondays, we pray for all our missionaries, 54 so far. We keep cards for all the families we know.—*Lissa*

♥ I expect them all to listen and be quiet during story time. They can ask questions, but I insist they pay attention. When they were too young or fidgety, we would just say prayers or sing Jesus Loves Me and put them in the crib before devotions (so they wouldn't be a distraction). It's kind of a "right of passage" when they're old enough to sit and listen to devotions.—*Shannon*

♥ Sometimes the littlest ones will still be asleep, but if they're awake, they're sitting with us.—*Karina*

♥ Since we usually do this during meals, we wait until mostly everyone is finished, but those who are still eating are allowed to continue.—*Ann*

♥ The kids are allowed to finish their breakfast while my husband reads the devotion. We also let the older ones take turns saying the prayer after devotion time. They can also ask questions about the story or Psalm, and both my husband and I offer answers.—*Kate*

♥ Our littlest ones are in the same room as all of us, but usually on the floor playing.—*Janet*

♥ Sometimes, they're allowed to color. I've noticed devotion does go better if we do it at breakfast. But when we do that, the baby is still sleeping.—*Dana*

♥ Everyone participates! No eating is allowed because we are usually in the family room with carpet. But, coloring, drawing, or writing is definitely allowed. We train them to listen well and think of one question to ask.—*Tina*

♥ Not usually, although I think it would be good if I had a special toy box for my younger ones for when our devotions go longer.—*Harriet*

♥ We gather everyone together for our family worship time. We do not bring any toys or snacks. We all sit together in the living room, the little ones on our laps. We explain that it is time for family worship and we're going to be still and quiet and listen to what Daddy has to share with us. When we are faithful to do this regularly, the children get very accustomed to this and it is a normal part of their routine! We keep it pretty short, 20 or 30 minutes, so that it's not necessary for toys or snacks.—*Laurie*

♥ Yes! Babies on laps. Sometimes kids are finishing meals during the readings and a toddler may play or wander, but generally it's short enough and good practice for sitting still in church.—*Reba*

♥ All three of our older children participate, and the baby just crawls and walks around and plays during this time.—*Sarah*

How do you handle getting through church services or Bible study with many little ones?

♥ Everyone takes a Bible and notepaper and a pencil. The younger ones draw a picture of something the pastor says. The next older ones will write single words that the pastor says. The next older group will write full quotations from the pastor or Scripture references. The oldest will take full notes. This keeps everyone occupied and listening! Also, prayer! If a child is distracting to others, I take him or her out and handle the situation. This is my job, and I take it seriously when it comes to church.—*Lissa*

♥ My husband and I used to do a "split shift" and leave the baby and toddlers at home, especially for Mass. Now, he doesn't attend church very much and I take them to my Bible church. They usually have Children's Church during the message. When they were really small, I'd bring things for them to do—usually coloring worked best. Sitting them on my lap was helpful, too. I'd always hope they'd fall asleep!—*Shannon*

♥ Practice "sit-time" at home. Start with 10 minutes a day, where they can look at Bible story books, and then slowly add time. Praise and reward them. This is a skill they need to learn for many things in life. Start early on. They can look at books but they may not talk and they may not get off their chair.—*Karina*

♥ I don't allow any toys or playthings. Only those who are able to read may get a bulletin or hymnal. Everyone is expected to stand and sit and pray with the congregation, and participate to the best of their ability. I'm pretty strict in church, but it has paid off. Anyone who acts up gets taken out and disciplined. Leaving the service is never pleasant for them. Since my husband is a pastor and I'm handling everyone by myself, it's really important for them to know what's expected and have me follow through. —*Ann*

♥ It all comes down to the tone that we've chosen for discipline in the household. My husband and I have always enacted loving discipline, and we are strict. However, every time a child is disciplined, we follow up with forgiveness and a hug and a kiss. This lays the groundwork for our experiences out and about, traveling, and at church. The discipline that we've established is a big part of the reason that we can travel as much as we do, enjoy a pretty flexible schedule, and know that the children are going to have fun, too. I've never been the type to take toys or snacks to church. I think that sends the message, "Adults are supposed to listen, but you can play or eat in here." It's God's house, not our home! The kids are expected to sit. I find that they challenge me the most when they're 18 months to 3 years old and that's when I have to lay it on the line. I've had several tests with each of the children, but we've learned together, and they are very well-behaved in church. Part of the reason I need this from them is that my husband never has the chance to sit with us. If a 2-year-old is being naughty, talking to her hours later is pointless and unfair. I need to enforce our rules, not expect anyone else to do it. The last reason I need the children to know how to behave in church is because I play organ about half of the Sundays. If they won't behave for me, they certainly won't behave for a friend! If I let my kids behave like animals in church, that takes away my opportunity to serve the Lord through music. So, the loving discipline that comes from the Lord is a comfort to all of us; My husband and I are enabled through the Spirit to serve during the church service, knowing that the children are not going to detract from the Word by anything they'll do. And don't get me wrong; I'm not saying it always goes perfectly, but many people make a point to tell us, "Your children are so well-behaved in church." —*Kate*

♥ Our babies have always stayed with us in church for their first year. The 2- and 3-year-olds are in the nursery as we work with them to learn to sit quietly for service time. Then, from age 4 on, they are with our family in the sanctuary. For the non-readers, we have special notebooks that they use to copy words from the Bible or that I have written, draw pictures related to the message or quietly "read" through their Bibles. I do use faith-based stickers to reward their participation in worship, which they put on their notebooks. For the older children, they are encouraged to copy the Scripture passage that was taught or take notes from the sermon. At home, we all discuss the sermon and ask the younger children questions.—*Janet*

♥ We have found it really helpful to train for church. I line up chairs and put on a tape recording of the Bible for 20 minutes. All the children are expected to sit still as if in church. If they did not, I could discipline them more immediately than I could at church. After a while, they all did really well. The baby sits on my lap.—*Amy*

Editor's Note: I have found Amy's "church practice" tip to be really helpful for our family!

♥ My children have their own church classes that they attend, but I keep the youngest with me until at least one year of age.—*Sharon*

♥ We have never used the nursery, other than to change a diaper! I used the "cry room" to nurse a fussy baby. Otherwise, we kept the dear children in church or walked the back hallway where we could still usually hear the service via a speaker system. We did allow snacks sometimes, but wasn't a regular occurrence, nor were toys. They just learned to sit during the preaching, and we encouraged them to join in with the group parts.—*Karol*

♥ I like our children to be with us, but I leave it up to my husband. I always have my nursing baby with me until about 2 years of age. Then, they start going to Sunday School with an older sibling. We have children in Sunday School until about grade 3 or 4, and then they come back into church with the adults. We feel they get more out of the Sunday School lesson from 3 years to 9 years. At about 9 years, they are ready to listen and gain wisdom from the adult message. This has worked for us because of our church set-up.—*Tina*

♥ My children were allowed to bring crayons, coloring books, and toys to church until they were 3. Once they turned 3, they could bring one doll or stuffed animal, but were expected to sit and pay attention through the whole service, although I did let them stay asleep if they happened to fall asleep. Once they turned 4, they were no longer allowed to bring anything to church and were expected to stay awake throughout the whole service.—*Lyn*

♥ We sometimes use snacks at church or Bible studies for the smallest ones. We also sometimes allow quiet toys and coloring or drawing. The smallest ones are often on Mom or Dad's lap for easier management.—*Laurie*

♥ Church is a struggle! I'm usually in the "Catechetical Nursery" we have set up at our church. We moms sit in the back room, with a big window, and try to teach/talk/catechize our kids through the service. During the sermon, we moms try to listen while the little ones clamor about. We have a student who keeps the children who are 4 and under in the nursery during Bible Class. The other children sit with parents during Bible class and quietly color or play with puzzles. When my son turns 4, I'm not sure he's going to be capable of sitting for Bible class. I may have to throw in the towel and go home after services, as I did before. We'll see.—*Reba*

♥ I bring books or a snack to keep the little ones occupied. Many times, we end up in the cry-room. Kids will learn to sit still eventually. The older kids help with the younger ones, and sometimes people from church help.—*Betty*

Do you pray with each child before bed?

♥ We all pray as a family in the living room at night before bed.—*Sheri*

♥ We pray after family worship, and then we tuck them each in bed individually.—*Lissa*

♥ I do it if Daddy isn't around, but this has become a special time for them. I'm done by the end of the day. So is he, and he often just falls asleep with them, but that's okay, too.—*Karina*

♥ Bedtime is, thankfully, Daddy's time. I read the bedtime story and then he brushes teeth and says prayers with everyone, usually the Lord's Prayer, the Creed, and Luther's Evening Prayer. I say goodnight and give hugs and kisses afterward.—*Ann*

♥ We don't do this individually. We say Luther's Evening Prayer together with all of them together, allow each to add their own extemporaneous prayers, sing a hymn, and have kisses all around. —*Kate*

♥ My husband blesses each of our children and prays over them every night. John Piper—Desiring God Ministries (*4)—has a wonderful booklet and set of blessing cards that has served as a tool for this special time each night.—*Janet*

♥ Daddy does that—maybe a small devotion with all, then prayers, sometimes separate with the boy and the girls.—*Dana*

♥ Honestly, I don't, although I should take more time to pray for, and with, my children.—*Sharon*

♥ This is not necessarily an "every night, every child" occurrence, but most nights either my husband or myself or both of us spend time in the children's bedroom praying, teaching, and talking with them. And at least once a week, we lay down with all of them and "soak" in worship music.—*Karol*

♥ We pray with all of our children either together or individually every night depending on if the baby is crying or what the other needs are. They will remind us if we are occupied with another child—they won't let us forget to pray with them!—*Tina*

♥ We all start our day praying together as a family and end our day praying together as a family.—*Lyn*

♥ My husband usually puts the children to bed at night. He takes time, if possible, to read to them for a few minutes before tucking everyone in to bed. He then takes time to pray with them and allow them time to pray as well!—*Laurie*

♥ I pray in the doorway of their room.—*Diana*

♥ Yes, my husband and I always say prayers with our children and tuck them in before bed.—*Mery*

♥ I do get the kids ready for bed and say prayers with all of them. After our hugs and kisses, the kids usually listen to music, books on tape, or the *Listening to Luther* CD (*5).—*Reba*

♥ We all kneel beside the bed and pray together. Then, they all crawl into bed and we give each of them hugs and kisses. If they have questions, then we talk a bit. After we leave the room, they are given freedom to sing or talk quietly until they fall asleep. There have been some times when they've felt the need for extra cuddle time. So, I've sat by their bed and had them each take a turn cuddling on my lap for a bit more prayer time.—*Sarah*

Big families are wonderful because ...

♥ ... there is never a dull moment! You can change the world for Christ! No two days are the same!—*Sheri*

♥ ... God created and crafted each and every one of these precious children and we want all the little blessings He wants to give us! How humbling that God has given me my beloved husband and my precious children.—*Lissa*

♥ ... there is never a dull moment. My kids don't have to ever worry about finding someone to play with. My kids learn to stand up for themselves and be heard. They learn to be individuals and compete for what they want, or back down if needed. My kids learn to pick their battles. My kids learn that they cannot have everything they want. My kids learn to obey because Mommy and Daddy don't have the time to say it twice. They will never be lonely and there will always be someone to lend a hand or to lead the way. We are almost guaranteed to have a house full of grandchildren visiting someday!—*Shannon*

♥ ... there is so much love and excitement and opportunity to show Christ's love within the family and without. Big families stand out in today's society just by being big! Use the opportunity to be a blessing to others.—*Karina*

♥ ... it's so exciting to see the older children helping and loving the younger ones. Every time we have a baby, the whole dynamic changes and each person has something different to offer.—*Ann*

♥ ... they provide a safe, loving atmosphere for kids. They teach Mom and Dad to put others first. There's always someone to talk to or play with. They support each other in their walk with the Lord.—*Kate*

♥ ... children are a heritage from the Lord, a gift! They provide a means to bring our homes joy and are the means, at times, that the Lord uses to grow us and change us for His purposes.—*Janet*

♥ ... any size family is wonderful if they are serving the Lord God with all their hearts. The size of the family doesn't matter. It's being content with what God will give you and making Him Lord of your life in all areas.—*Amy*

♥ ... there's never a dull moment!—*Dana*

♥   ... I have to keep dealing with my selfishness. I have to keep allowing God to strengthen me. I don't ever get to think I can do this well without His daily help. It is great for my kids because they learn patience, sharing, and working together as a family. They also have built-in life-long friends.—*Christy*

♥   ... they are God's gift. I will always have some family around, and if I get old and decrepit, I'm more likely to have family to help me.—*Sharon*

♥   ... God builds them, and all that He creates is very good.—*Karol*

♥   ... there are more hugs and love!—*Tina*

♥   ... you always have someone to talk to.—*Harriet*

♥   ... God gave each child to us in His perfect timing! There are few things that I am sure of, but this is one.—*Diana*

♥   ... the children always have someone to play with. It is never boring.—*Mery*

♥   ... you are surrounded by people who love each other. The kids always have someone to play with and they learn to get along with others in a good environment. In a big family, you have more people you can count on.—*Betty*

♥   ... when you're a widow, you won't be alone.—*Reba*

♥   ... there's never a dull moment; everyone has lots of playmates; the energy and creative juices run high; there's ample opportunity for everyone to learn relationship and teamwork skills; and one day we'll be able to have our own musical band and informal sports team just with our own family!—*Sarah*

♥   ... eternity, baby! I'm taking them along, God-willing.—*Betsy*

Wisdom of Mature Moms

"[Train] the older women likewise, that they be reverent in behavior, not slanderers, not given to much wine, teachers of good things—that they admonish the young women to love their husbands, to love their children, to be discreet, chaste, homemakers, good, obedient to their own husbands, that the word of God may not be blasphemed."
Titus 2:3–5

The mothers featured in the body of this book are "in the trenches" of motherhood. Several mothers whose children are fully grown reminded me of "big picture" questions that needed to be asked. They responded with encouragement and advice. My heart goes out to the following mothers of many: Cheryl B., Sandy S., Julie Q., Joslyn M., Karen B., Susan G., Frances F., Amanda M., and my late Great Aunt LaVerne. Thank you from the bottom of my heart for your examples and wisdom!

Big families are wonderful because ...

♥ ... they give each other strength when it is needed, laughs when times are sad, and hugs every day. Each child is a unique individual, something like his or her siblings, but offering something to the world and to the family that no one else can give.

♥ ... each child is a gift from God! These wonderful little beings are our reminder of all those He loves and calls His own. I love my children because of who they've helped me become. I am not the same person that I was in my 20s!

♥ ... they are a picture of God's handiwork. Through them, we learn endless possibilities for relationships, support, creativity, self-reliance, self-sacrifice, service, and strength. A large family is a complex social network that is deep, fulfilling, and interconnected. We are provided for and we provide. When one falls, another picks us up. We learn that we can do without many things people think they must have: a room of one's own, dawdling in the bathroom, new clothes, and the latest gadgets. We learn to share what we have and not to focus on ourselves.

♥ ... they are able to provide the support for other family members. More members in a family keeps the family from getting bored and keeps them on a God-fearing course. Chores are shared and life is never lonely.

♥ ... for the children: they develop relationships with each other and life-long friendships that are special and different from all others; they learn to respect others by dealing with their siblings on a daily basis; they will have several other siblings to help them with the care and decision-making when their parents age.

♥ ... for the parents: The pleasure it brings is priceless! To give children new life experiences, to watch their personalities develop, to teach them about their Savior, to watch their faith grow and see it in action, to have so many loved ones to share life's experiences with, both good and bad. Truly gifts from God! To know that as you age there will be many loving hands to help you and many loving hearts to love you and pray for you.

♥ ... there are more people around to love and be involved in each other's lives.

♥ ... as they grow, they become your friends as well as your children. They also learn to care for others and not just themselves. Sharing is also something that children from a large family do more automatically.

♥ ... they give you such joy and pleasure as you see them raising their own families. The love and attention from grandchildren is so rewarding!

♥ ... when they are small, they are fun (mostly) to care for. It's exciting to watch them learn, to teach them, to know their friends. As adults, they are wonderful companions.

What pieces of equipment would you recommend to mothers currently raising big families in order to make their lives easier? Why?

♥ I don't remember any one piece of equipment that was a great help, other than backpacks for carrying my twins—one each for my husband and me—and of course the double stroller that my mom found at a yard sale.

♥ I do have a dishwasher now, but I didn't in the beginning; I was very thankful when we did get one! I also enjoy having a microwave, because I wasn't always "organized" for planning meals. Other than that, we tried different approaches to things all the time. I can't tell you how many times I literally moved the "toy room" because the toys always seemed to take over the rooms they were in! Finally, I tried to do what my mom had done for many years. She always packed away half the toys and then, every few months, when the six of us kids would get bored, she'd magically find all the hidden ones and it was like Christmas! Don't ever be afraid of trying new ideas. You'll never know until you try!

> ♥ **Editor's Note:** We love the suggestion of having a majority of the toys packed away. Each week, we rotate through a "new" set of toys. This keeps them fresh and exciting!

♥ There needs to be a place for the children to run, to work off their energy, whether it's 'round and 'round in the house, in the backyard, or in a park. Projects are important as the children get older, so they can focus their energy on something productive and rewarding. The home should look lived in. Regular mealtimes when you all sit down together, wholesome food, and adequate sleep are very important for health and a sense of security and order.

♥ I would recommend good devotion books and Bible story books. In the kitchen, a large mixer with dough hooks, if you enjoy making bread.

♥ A dishwasher will save time for other more important things. A vegetable garden and a freezer to store the produce will result in healthier and better tasting produce, and it will save you money. It's also a great experience for children. They love helping plant and pick and will also eat more veggies if they've helped to grow them, especially fresh peas, strawberries, and carrots straight from the garden.

♥ I'd recommend a deep freeze and maybe even a second refrigerator. These help cut down on trips to the grocer, and lets you buy in bulk to save money. After we'd been parents for 23 years, we began to realize that nearly all our friends had two refrigerators. We had a bigger family than they did and we lived much further from the grocery store! My husband is a pastor, and we lived next door to church, where the huge fridge sat empty most of the time. We got permission to start using it. That made it so much easier to buy more produce and to have a place to store 6 gallons of milk.

♥ Get a front pack/baby sling so your hands are free to deal with older children and baby feels secure and settled. Big toy boxes are handy; A room can be tidied up very quickly if all the toys are thrown into there. Develop routines. Having the children in bed by 7 p.m. gives you time with your husband and time to unwind from the day to do your thing, be it a quite time in the Word or a relaxing hobby. (People used to tell me that they could not get their kids to bed so early, but I always maintained that we as parents *put* them to bed. When they were babies, they got used to the routine.) Even now, our 16-year-old has an 8:30 p.m. bed time on school nights.

♥ I think garage sales and thrift stores are a wonderful boon for mothers these days. They weren't around when our children were young. Dishwashers are a big help, too, or use paper plates.

♥ I recommend a heavy-duty mixer, a vegetable chopper, a dishwasher, and any labor saving device that leaves parents with more time and energy to care for their children.

Do you have any regrets about how you spent your time during your children's growing years? What would you recommend to mothers with young children?

♥ I went back to teaching when my first son was less than a year old, so his babysitter got to potty train him and see a lot of the early learning. I was there for all of that with the other children. There were good and bad things about each situation. If you can stay home with your children while they are small, do it, but if you have to be out working, do your best and don't beat yourself up about it. Just leave it behind when you come home, and enjoy the kids when you are together. Don't use all of your at time at home cleaning and catching up on housework.

♥ I really enjoyed not having to work outside the home with our first two children. With our third, I started volunteering, and by the fourth child, I was working a full-time job so we could buy a home. I regret that I wasn't around as much for the last child. But you have to do what you have to do. When those regrets set in, I try to tell myself to have faith that God is in control of my children, whether I am present or not. But, I was always pretty picky about who was with our children. And to me, that was just common sense! We were blessed with good neighbors and friends. Another gift from God! Realize that just because you are legally an adult, you're not done being formed into whom God wants you to be. Don't be afraid to "grow up" a little more with your kids. There's so much to learn! Another thought: really try to learn about your kids. Just when you think you have them figured out, you don't! Pick yourself up, dust yourself off, and start again!

♥ What would I do differently? I would take the time to listen more and converse more deeply, especially with the boys. I would be less insecure about what I had to offer my children.

♥ I was very happy I could be a stay-at-home mom, and would recommend it to any family that could afford it. They were very happy years.

♥ I am so thankful I was home when children were small. I think home jobs are the best way to supplement income.

♥ I regret not spending more time with some of our children in the garden. Remember, the dust and cleaning will always be there, but the children will grow up and leave home. There are things that need to be done like laundry, meals, and yes, some cleaning, but remember to prioritize people above things. Sometimes you and the children both need a break from home. Go for a walk, to a park or playground, to the zoo, to visit a friend or relative with children, for an ice cream treat. It's amazing how getting away can stop the fighting, complaining, and whining and give everyone a new outlook!

♥ I should have been more diligent in teaching them chores. Not that I didn't do it, but not as well as I should have. I also didn't know that you can *teach* children to sing! Most of our kids learned to sing naturally, without training. It came easily to them. But the two that didn't could have been taught if I'd known that it was possible and if I'd known how. I also regret how much time I let them watch TV or use the computer. My kids didn't veg in front of a screen as much as the average American child. But it was still too much. And I got more lax with the younger kids due to the older kids' influence with regard to movies or activities. On the whole, though, I spent a lot of time with the kids. We homeschooled, and that allowed us enough time together, so that I am not pining for the days when they were young, days that I missed. I didn't miss those times together because we were living them, and had "time with the kids" to the full. Also, don't put too much in the schedule. Allow plenty of down-time, plenty of play-time, and plenty of veg-time. If the kids go to school, don't have them in sports *and* music *and* other activities.

♥ I have an embroidery picture I made when our third child was born. It said, "Scrubbing and cleaning can wait till tomorrow / 'Cause babies grow up I've learnt to my sorrow / So fly away cobwebs and dust, go to sleep / I'm rocking my baby and babies don't keep."

♥ If you are financially able to stay home with your children, that is a great positive for them. My eldest son told me at his age of 45 years old that he hated the day that I went to back to work. He said he thought about it all the day long at school! That made me feel very bad.

♥ I was a stay-at-home mom who "earned" money by canning, baking, sewing, and haircutting. For recreation, I had 10 piano students. I enjoyed my time immensely.

Having already raised a number of children, what advice do you have for today's mothers of big families?

♥ Rejoice in the privilege of watching these amazing new people grow and develop into terrific adults that you will love to have for friends.

♥ I am going to share a saying that my oldest sister has told me on days when I was ready to pull out my hair. She would lean over and whisper in my ear, "Just keep telling yourself, 'They do grow up, they do grow up!'" It not only brought a smile to my face; but got me through some rough times. And you know what? She was right. They've grown up to be some wonderful people!

♥ The comments I hear from overwhelmed mothers who don't feel like they can possibly do any more than what they're already doing are from women with two or three young ones and no older children. That seems to be the roughest time. But I've noticed that if you hang in there, they do grow up, and the older children begin to help carry the load. Even entertaining the baby, or emptying the dishwasher, or setting the table, or answering the phone, or running errands, or bringing the diaper, or picking up are all huge supports for a busy mom. Children can take on their share of responsibility and it makes a world of difference. While no one's situation is identical, the time of having a few small children at home may be most demanding. You might get that especially needy child, but each new baby doesn't automatically multiply your work again. The demands actually become more manageable as your family grows if children have learned they are an essential part of making it work. When children learn obedience to parents, care and respect for one another, love for the Lord, and find their valued place in a secure family structure, they are part of a team. A large family needs order and it needs love. Everyone should know what is expected of them.

♥ Don't be afraid or feel guilty about getting some assistance, even if it's with the laundry, cleaning, cooking, baking, baby-changing or whatever. Help is a good thing until your children are able to be of more assistance. Even a little assistance on a regular basis goes a long way.

♥ Stay home with them! Find a hobby that inspires you. Doing daycare is not for everyone, but I did enjoy it and my children enjoyed the friends.

♥ Remember the importance of daily prayer for guidance for both you and the children. Keep the lines of communication open, especially as children enter their teens. Don't be a dictator; really listen to them. Speak lovingly, but be firm.

♥ They grow up in stages. Keep reminding yourself, "This too shall pass." Promote respect and love for their siblings; children are selfish by nature and need guidance to think of others. This comes with time, so don't give up. Teach them to say special prayers for each other at bedtime in their own words.

♥ Stay the course! The rewards will come in the love of your children and grandchildren and great-grandchildren!

♥ If you see a behavior problem in your child, confront it immediately. Don't wait for someone else to discover it or solve it.

♥ If life with several children seems too difficult, maybe you need to simplify your life in some other way so that you have the energy to keep up with the kids. Maybe if you're involved with lots of other activities, you might have to say "no" for a while, until your other priorities are at a level that don't cause so much stress. This can be very difficult at times. But if you are stressed, the kids can feel that. I also know it's important to have time for yourself. This doesn't have to be elaborate, but, do you find things like going for a walk help you unwind? Then make time to do that! For me, I enjoy sewing and crafting. Once a month, I looked forward to going to "craft night." There, I could enjoy my friends and we would share things like raising kids, recipes, patterns, etc. It was only once a month and my husband was always willing to let me have that time away. I never understood how he didn't need some time like that. But, maybe his work was all he needed? I don't know. But he never complained about me going. And it sure helped! It was like going to church once a week. I needed to start a fresh week of being a mom, wife, and housekeeper. No matter what happened last week, I knew I was ready to face the next.

♥ Most of all, moms need the support, encouragement, and help of their husbands. He needs to let you talk about the challenges you face. And you need daily family devotions from the beginning. Teach the children to read early and provide them with good reading material. They will expand their horizons independently and be occupied for hours on end!

♥ It seems to me that the mothers who miss their kids most when they are grown are either the moms who sent their kids to school (and thus had only off-school time together), or those who had just one or two kids. It's almost like there is a certain amount of "mothering" that's in each of us and it needs to be spent. If it's not spent by the time the youngest is all grown up, then the mom misses the kids more. But the moms who really have plenty of time with the kids can begin to move on with other aspects of life, while still loving their kids deeply. Mothers are not "bad" if they don't fuss over the baby's milestones or get involved with every little thing. We live in a society where there is just way too much fawning over children and childhood. We all know that there is too much consumerism going on out there. Kids have too many toys, too much TV, too much computer, too many clothes, too many treats, too many cool vacations, too much stuff altogether. We know that Americans have the monetary resources to totally spoil kids. We know that we shouldn't spoil kids. But we just keep doing it because we don't want to deny them any advantage. The problem is, paradoxically, by lavishing things on them, we are denying them something even more important—the need to work, the lesson of learning to wait, the resourcefulness that comes from doing without, etc. But few of us have the self-discipline to deny our children all those things when we have the monetary ability to provide those things. That's why there is a significant blessing in poverty! Even our poverty in this country is filthy rich compared to most people throughout the world and throughout history. Our so-called poverty today forces us to deny our children things that they ought to be denied, but which we may not have the heart to deny.

If we can understand the concept when it comes to *stuff*, we ought to understand the analogy when it comes to *time*, too. Now, don't get me wrong. I think it's very important to spend time with kids, to be available to help them when they need it, to give hugs, to dawdle over post-meal conversation, to go on errands together, and do chores together. But children also need to learn to entertain themselves. And they need to learn that the world does not revolve around them. If your need to straighten the house, to make a nice dinner for your husband, to have a hobby of your own, or whatever it is, if those things help the children learn that they are not the center of the universe, then your "neglect" of them serves a good purpose.

♥ Ask for help! Find a person you can telephone and say, "May I bring my children over to play while I grocery shop, freeze corn, help at church?" Don't be afraid to ask. But don't expect your "grandmas" to know when to volunteer. Ask her (or him) and they'll say yes or no and love your children as their own. Everywhere I've lived, I had someone who helped us. Sometimes, these "grandmas" get tired easily, so short periods work best. Hire someone occasionally to clean.

♥ I would like to share a prayer with you that I found when my children were young. I prayed it often.

> O heavenly Father, make me a better parent. Teach me to understand my children, to listen patiently to what they have to say, and to answer all their questions kindly. Keep me from interrupting them or contradicting them. Make me as courteous to them as I would have them be to me. Forbid that I should ever laugh at their mistakes or resort to shame or ridicule when they displease me. May I never punish them for my own selfish satisfaction or to show my power. Let me not tempt my child to lie or steal. And, guide me hour by hour that I may demonstrate by all I say and do that honesty produces happiness. Reduce, I pray, the meanness in me. And when I am out of sorts, help me, O Lord, to hold my tongue. May I ever be mindful that my children are children and I should not expect of them the judgment of adults. Let me not rob them of the opportunity to wait on themselves and to make decisions. Bless me with the bigness to grant them all their reasonable requests and the courage to deny them privileges I know will do them harm. Make me fair and just and kind. And fit me, O Lord, to be loved and respected and imitated by my children. Amen.

What are your words of encouragement for mothers of large families who are struggling and feel burdened?

♥ *Everybody* is burdened with something, but not everybody's burden will bring the overwhelming joy and rewards of raising your children.

♥ Take it to the Lord in prayer!

♥ Don't listen to those who act like being overwhelmed is a sign from Heaven that you're not doing the right thing. What an incredible loss of God's immeasurable gifts for us to say we are not able to handle any more children! He offers life. He also provides the way. Many things He calls us to are terribly difficult. Do we say no? Of course, we don't. We say, "He will provide." I will tell you without hesitation, that the rewards far exceed the times of trouble. The rewards are immeasurable, and even inexplicable. Many people will never know that deep and abiding richness of a large family who walks in His way. I am more blessed than I have any right to be. I don't say too much about it, because I don't want it to in any way diminish small families, especially since in some cases, it's not by their design. But they have no idea what they've missed. There is just no end to the blessings! And how I came to it is a mystery to me, except that He is lavish in His graces.

♥ Remember, there is no such person as a perfect mom. We're all sinful human beings doing our best with God's help. Daily prayer is so important. Always go to the Lord first before you throw up your arms and say, "I can't handle this!" Organize! Daily life flows more smoothly when children know what to expect when. Prioritize chores and meals. Establish a regular bedtime. They need the routine and you need a little time for yourself in the evening to unwind from the day. Find joy in everyday things and remember to laugh; it works wonders! I know a mom of 14 children who turned her children's attitudes around by laughing with them instead of trying to solve each complaint and disagreement they had with each other. Remember that kids are resilient and forgiving. A few mistakes on our part won't ruin them for life. They often forget more quickly than we do.

♥ These children are the work God has given you to do in life. His blessing will be on your efforts, and even on your failures. When you are burdened, when you are struggling, when you can't do for your family what you know you should do, go to confession and hear Jesus' words of love for you. Hear Him declare you to be the perfect mother, because keeping your eyes on Him and receiving His forgiveness is the only thing that changes your heart and your will to be more like the mother you long to be.

> ♥ **Editor's Note:** Are there any more lovely and comforting words? Copy this down and stick it somewhere for a beautiful reminder of the truth!

♥ Every time you have to get up at night or change a diaper, just remember you are one day closer to not having to do it and one day, that child will be older and not need so much of your energy. Your baby is your greatest masterpiece. It is a beautiful reflection of the love God pours on us through our marriage. And as much as you love your child, God loves him or her even more, and knows *exactly* what your child needs.

♥ Trust in the Lord, who knows your needs! He will supply the needed strength and understanding to get through each day!

Appendix Two

Editor's Answers, 2010

I'm certainly no expert in raising a large family—I don't even fit the criteria to answer my own survey with only 3 children! But, I have thoughtfully considered these questions, and made changes to our lives based on the mentoring of the moms in the book. Enjoy my bumbling!

Domestic Tranquility

Which kitchen items help you feed your large family efficiently?

♥ I use our 6-quart non-stick pan daily. I also use our blender every day for breakfast smoothies with the children's vitamins deceptively added in! I might have to look into larger capacity blenders, though! Though I don't own them, I think that several dozen non-stick muffin pans would be wonderful. When we make muffins, we make dozens and keep extra in the freezer for a quick snack.

♥ We're only working with a family of 5 so far, but since I double or triple most meals, I already feel that my "kitchen-ware" is reaching capacity! Early on in our marriage, before children, I wished I would have had a toaster oven. I certainly didn't need the regular-sized oven for just the two of us. But now, when I'm baking bread and making a few casseroles, even our large oven doesn't seem to have enough room!

Do you plan meal menus ahead of time? How do you know that you'll have enough? Do you ration?

♥ My latest menu-planning "kick" is to choose three meals for the week and double them all. When I do my monthly shopping for all of the staples, I've already planned the monthly meals. I buy

155

everything except fresh fruits, veggies, milk, and eggs. Usually, for each week, I plan a nicer meal for Sunday Dinner (like a roast or fish) and two plain meals (like something vegetarian or a soup). If, after doubling the meals, we still need more food for the week, I whip up some scrambled eggs and pancakes as a dinner. For lunch all week, we have leftovers from dinner, or something quick and easy—tuna sandwiches, hard-boiled eggs, or baked potatoes. Snacks usually consist of apples and peanut butter, homemade granola bars, muffins, yogurt and oats, or something else with protein, fruit, and starch. Our process for serving the children is to give them a few spoonfuls of everything that is being served. We give them a reasonable amount for their age and they are expected to eat all of it. After that, they are allowed to request more of any of the foods, though usually I will not serve them more fruit. If they ask for more, they must finish it before they are excused from the table. Our children each have a sippy cup of milk in the fridge, from which they may drink at any time between meals.

Do your children snack on what they want when they want to, or do you have specific times and foods?

♥ Their milk cups are always available in the fridge. This is my "go-to" when they whine about being hungry between meals. Even in the rare case that they have leftovers in the fridge from the previous meal, I usually don't let them get them out if it isn't meal-time. Since my children are still all young, I feel like I need to supervise them when they are eating—for safety and cleanliness.

How do you clean up effectively after a meal (especially if you have one or more children in high chairs or booster seats)?

♥ Our children have their "jobs" to complete after each meal: folding their napkins, picking up crumbs, pushing in their chairs, and clearing their dishes from the table. Although I'd like this process to run smoothly, it is usually like pulling teeth! I'm constantly reminding them, even though we've been doing this over a year, and they have a chore chart on the wall made with photographs of them completing each job! After these jobs are done, sometimes my oldest offers to wash the table, or I ask her to help me with the dishes. In the evenings, the children get ready for bed with my husband right after dinner, so I usually clean up the table/floor/high-chairs at that time. Often during the day, I don't get the table washed or crumbs picked up, but I'm sure that will need to change when we use the table for school more frequently.

Lots of children means lots of dishes. How do they get done?

♥ Usually, after breakfast, my husband washes the smoothie dishes and the blender by hand, while I nurse the baby or finish getting ready for the day. Lunch and snack dishes are pretty minimal during the day; sometimes I'll wash them in the afternoon during nap time. Other times, I just let them sit until the dinner dishes. After supper, sometimes my husband or I will load the dishwasher. Sometimes I wash them while he gets the children ready for bed. Sometimes we do them together after the children are asleep. I hope to train the children soon to help with the dishes as part of their "jobs." I guess I'll wait until they've masted clearing the table!

At what ages are children capable of helping around the house? Do you have your children participate in these ways?

♥ I'm definitely still learning this one! In the years between when I wrote this survey and now, our oldest was diagnosed with special needs. In some ways, I'm still not sure what the average child can be expected to do at a certain age because our oldest is atypical. As the years go by, I hope to have the children acquiring more skills to help around the house. Right now, my focus is to equip them with a heart to serve so they ask me and Daddy how they can help. This is sometimes hard, though, because they often make more work when they "help"! It sure is a learning process!

♥ We try to have "family house cleaning" twice a week on Mondays and Thursdays when Daddy comes home from work. I've learned through experience that I really don't get much hardcore cleaning done during the day with little ones underfoot. I try to keep things picked up, but I'm not able to deep-clean the kitchen, wash the fan blades, or organize the closets like I can when he is home. During these cleaning times, we try to have the girls "help" by spraying and wiping the windows or dusting with one parent while the other gets some major cleaning done. We also attempt to vacuum and sweep on those days. I have a weekly/monthly/yearly master checklist of when chores should ideally be done, but I sure haven't been following that! Someday, when the children take on more responsibility, I'll hand over that checklist!

♥ We're also working hard at having the children perform the basic procedures in the home, such as putting their dirty clothes in the laundry, putting their clean clothes in their drawers, hanging up their towels after their baths, taking off and putting away their shoes and coats when we enter the house, and other common routines.

How can you keep up with the laundry?

♥ This is getting harder and harder, but I think it will get easier in a few years as the children are able to take over their own laundry! Right now, I usually start the laundry Thursday night. My goals is to have all of it washed and put away by the end of the weekend! Honestly, I'm bad about sorting by colors or wash cycles. This is probably due to teaching myself how to do laundry in my high school dormitory laundromat! My basic routine consists of doing one load of adult dress clothes, one load of adult pajamas/underwear, and one load of children's clothes and towels. I strongly encourage all members of the family to re-wear clothes as much as possible before tossing them in the laundry.

How do you manage all of the diapers?

♥ I actually still have three in diapers every night! I've been all across the spectrum with the diapering situation! For now, we use disposables for everyone at night. During the day, the older two are in underwear and we clean up messes around the house as needed. The baby wears cloth during the day, but we usually change him to disposables if we leave the house. I have a cloth bag lining a garbage can next to the changing table where the dirty cloth diapers go. When it is full, or gets stinky enough that I feel sorry for the children sleeping in that room, I pick the liner up out of the can and bring it downstairs for a rinse cycle in the washer. Then, we add detergent (*1), change the cycle to hot water, and start it again. Finally, we hang our diapers on the indoor line in our laundry room or put them in the dryer, depending on the humidity in our house. We recently added magnets to the top of our washing machine so my husband and I can communicate about the status of the diapers. This has worked really well if my husband starts them before he goes to work, and I come across them during the day, not knowing if they are merely pre-rinsed or really clean.

How often do you go shopping for food? When do you buy other non-food necessities?

♥ When I wrote this question 2 years ago, I shopped twice a week for a family of four. Now, as I family of five, I can't seem to handle leaving the house that often! Usually I do one giant shopping trip per month and it takes place on the Saturday afternoon after pay-day. My husband stays home and entertains the children. I've gone back and forth about whether to plan menus monthly or weekly, since the ads come out weekly. I sometimes think that by menu-planning monthly, I'm losing out on the weekly deals for the three weeks when I'm not planning menus. But, over time, I've realized that, usually, that isn't the case. On the other three Saturdays, I usually still make a quick trip to the store to refresh our fruit and veggie supply, and I can purchase the fruits and veggies that are on sale. During that trip, too, if there is some extraordinary sale, I can also stock up on that item.

♥ For our household supplies, I generally buy those during my giant-once-a-month shopping trips. I also purchase our smoothie supplies and many vitamins online (*2), which has been a wonderful blessing since I can compare both nutritional information and cost per unit from the comfort of my office chair, rather than having to take the time to do it in the store!

Who goes shopping with you? Does it work well?

♥ I used to take the children with me during the day while my husband was at work. This was optimal because we could have family time together on the evenings and weekends. However, that was when I shopped once or twice a week. Recently, I took my children along for a monthly shopping trip. I *could not* fit all of the food in the cart with the children! It took all of my physical strength to haul them through the store not to mention all of the behaviors I had to deal with! I simply cannot do that on a monthly shopping trip again! I will take one, two, or even the whole family to the store on the weekend when it is just to replenish our fresh supplies, but for those monthly trips, my husband keeps them at home!

Money Matters

What are your money saving tips for shopping?

♥ I have one daughter who recently started a gluten-free diet. I've really tried to change the diet of our whole family so that I don't have to cook separately just for her. In some ways, this has saved us some money. I no longer buy bread or bakery items. Our store-bought snack items are limited (no Little Debbie snacks or Oreos). I always hear that vegetarian meals save money, but I'm not convinced that it's true. I mean, cheese can be $4 per pound around here, but if I check the sales, chicken breasts might be less than $2 per pound. I try not to plan our lunches around cheese (like grilled cheese or quesadillas), but rather chicken and veggies. In my menu plan, I don't specify certain fruits for snack or veggies for side dishes, but purchase whatever is on sale for that week. Some weeks, we might have a lot of pears and lettuce. Other weeks, we have apples and cucumbers. I've also noticed that sometimes, the same fruit in the organic section of our supermarket is on sale and cheaper than its conventional counterpart in the regular produce aisle!

Do you buy in bulk?

♥ For awhile we were members at a buyer's club, but we think we spent more money there than we would at a regular supermarket. Besides the fact that we shopped there for leisure, not just food and supplies, our club didn't have the generic brands that we could purchase elsewhere. For us, the buyer's club was not a good deal on the price-per-unit, although we got our money's worth on the samples! Many of the things that we use up quickly can't be bought in bulk and stored in our home (milk, eggs, fruit), but I do stock up on pantry items if I find an amazingly good deal on things like tomato sauce or applesauce. We usually do buy large bags of legumes and beans since we go through those quickly. We also are working our way through a 20-pound bag of brown rice which we keep in the deep freeze, and a 50-pound bag of popcorn from last year! Good thing I have a neighbor who will barter with me!

♥ I would like to be part of a family co-op in my area where we could order oats or flour, divide it among several families, and share the cost, but I don't know of any that exist in my area. Maybe after I'm done editing this book, I'll try to start something!

How do you manage to keep your family supplied with toiletries like shampoo, toothpaste, deodorant, and toilet paper, on a budget?

♥ It seems like I change the toilet paper roll every day! Is this unusual? Maybe we go through it so quickly since 3/5 of us are girls? The children are slowly learning to use an appropriate amount of toothpaste, soap, water, and shampoo. This isn't too difficult, yet, since my husband and I still completely oversee the children's hygiene routine.

How do you keep Christmas and birthdays special, but affordable?

♥ We just do small gifts in our children's stockings for Christmas, and buy the entire family one larger gift. Since they don't get much at Christmas, we maximize birthdays and give them several special gifts at that time. It's easier on the budget since the birthdays are spread throughout the year. It also keeps the focus of Christmas on Christ. I don't think that we'll really do "parties" for birthdays. We'll probably allow the children to pick a special family activity, like bowling or mini-golf, since we don't regularly do that type of thing.

How can you afford hair cuts for so many children?

♥ My oldest two children are girls and we are letting their hair grow out. My baby is a boy, but he doesn't have much hair yet. Thus, our total yearly budget for haircuts is $0.

Many moms in smaller families are religious about getting their children's photographs taken professionally. Is this something you do? Are there alternatives?

♥ We tried to do professional photos every few months with our first. But she cried every time, so I gave up! We have a lot of photos of the children without the professional portraits. I'd actually rather have a nice portrait of our whole family than each of them as individuals. With digital cameras becoming more common, I think it will become easier for parents to take their own photos and store them on the computer.

What are your ideas about whether or not children should receive allowance?

♥ I've been greatly influenced by the moms in this book! We do not plan to give our children allowance for helping us with our basic household tasks, although we do regularly put money away in an account for them, just as my husband's parents did for him. We will probably allow them to do extra jobs for us (such as gardening or washing the car) and be paid, or do those jobs for others and receive due compensation. But we don't plan to let them do whatever they want with that money. We want to budget with them and help them use it wisely by tithing, saving, and spending it only on things that are worthwhile, rather than frivolous.

What does your family do for cheap entertainment?

♥   We always have dessert after our Sunday dinner which is fun to both make and eat. Usually, I have ice cream on hand, and we'll serve that if we have spontaneous company. I hope in the future that we can help the children develop puppet shows and plays for cheap entertainment. We have done some camping, too, and will probably do more in the future!

♥   Our county is very good at offering a variety of programs and entertainment for free. We try take advantage of these opportunities (concerts in the park, outdoor movies, etc.). Since my husband teaches college, there are always events taking place on campus, and often we can attend these events for a reduced price. We all enjoy walking or biking. A big source of cheap entertainment for us is bargain hunting! I imagine that some types of volunteer work can also be just as entertaining as spending a lot of money!

Many families cite the high cost of college as a valid reason not to bring any more children into the world. Do you have a plan as far as college goes?

♥   We don't really have a plan. But, I'm sure God will provide.

Generally "Kid"ding Around

Are you able to keep your children's baby books current? Are there alternatives to the traditional baby book?

♥   I have a baby book for each child and I try to fill out some updates each time I pick up developed photos. Then, when I paste the photos in there, I jot down some notes. It isn't perfect and definitely doesn't have the specific dates when each child cut each tooth, but it's something! My husband and I also write in what we call their "baby journals." We start these when I am pregnant with each one and have continued to write a page or two every 2 or 3 months. I think that these will be more meaningful to the children than the baby books when they are adults. I love to look back and read what was important to all of use a few months or years ago.

What is your method of getting toys picked up?

Editor's Note: Apparently we didn't pick up toys in 2010, because there is no answer to this question.

How do you manage various appointments for all of your children? Who goes along with you?

♥ If my husband is working, then I take all three children with me. I find this to be extremely difficult. I feel discouraged reading some of the other moms who say to train your children at home, and then all will go well in public! We train them, prep them, and bring along entertainment, but going out in public with all three still feels like a zoo to me! However, I'm learning not to compare my children's behavior to others when we are out and about. I do my best to prepare and then roll with the punches! I've also learned that I care for them better if I myself am comfortable— which means wearing shorts to the doctor's office since they keep it at about 80 degrees, and always keeping water and a snack (for me!) in the diaper bag. I do feel responsible if my children are ill-mannered, as it may reflect badly both on large families and Christianity. But there's only so much I can do. And, by God's grace, the times I've been in public with them and had a witnessing opportunity, all three children were perfectly behaved!

How do you outfit all of your children?

♥ We are blessed with generous friends and neighbors, and my mom and aunt are bargain hunters! I have bought very few clothing items for my children, mostly just needing to supplement what we have been given with items like tights or underwear.

♥ I used to try to store every clothing item away for the next child based on season and size. But now, especially after reading some of the moms above, I have been giving away much more of it to families who would use it immediately. Donating some of it just spreads around God's blessings.

When it is time to leave the house, how do you make sure all of the children are clean?

♥ This is so haphazard! We try to get the children to the potty and change Baby's diaper about 10 minutes before we leave. We usually have the diaper bag stocked, but we still scramble for shoes and coats in the winter. Part of this is due to parking in the garage in the winter and using the side door, versus parking in the driveway in the summer and using the front door. Even Mom and Dad don't always know where shoes and coats are!

How do you get into and out of the house efficiently—hats, coats, shoes, bags?

♥ Near our side door, we have both an adult coat rack and a children's coat rack. Since installing the children's rack, getting out of the house has gone a lot more smoothly. They can reach (and put away) their own coats, and there are small cubby holes above the hooks into which they can shove mittens and hats. Our coat rack has a bench below it in which we store shoes. We arranged this room of the house in order to ease the indoor/outdoor transition, and I think it's been working fairly well, aside from the constant stepping over shoes. They still don't make it into the storage area!

How is your bathroom, and bathroom time, organized?

♥ We usually do baths with all three children in the tub at once on Wednesday afternoons and Saturday evenings. They each have one hooded towel, so they hang nicely on hooks in the children's bedroom. We bring the towels into the bathroom for baths and put them on the floor. Usually, the towels get washed on Fridays. I find it simpler to assign them each a specific towel, rather than having a supply of towels that anyone may use. My husband and I do our hygiene before the children wake up, so the potty is free for them when they first get up. Anticipating frustrations with bathroom time in the future, we are working on re-doing some aspects of our bathroom. All of the cabinets, drawers, and doors opened to the same point, and when pregnant, I could literally only squeeze through the opening! So, we've installed a pocket-door and added a laundry sink (to be used for tooth-brushing and hair-washing, not laundry) where our bathroom storage used to be. So far, we are very pleased with the results, although we have significantly less cabinet space. Fortunately, we were able to buy most of the remodel items inexpensively from a hardware thrift store.

What is the rooming situation with all of your children? Does it work well?

♥ Why, this seems to change every month or two! We have two bedrooms on our main floor. Our ideal would be to have my husband and me sleep in one bedroom and the three children sleep in the other. The children's bedroom is set up for this with an over-sized playpen and a bed with a trundle underneath it. However, once we moved the second child to the trundle, there was no getting to sleep for the older two. They'd sing and play (or tease and bother), which then kept the baby from falling asleep. Now, the younger two sleep in the children's bedroom and the oldest sleeps in the guest room downstairs, but still keeps all of her belongings in the room on the main floor. It works fine for now, but I'd like the sisters to learn to share a room eventually!

How do you find time to care for the physical needs of the baby (like feeding, bathing, and potty-training) while meeting the emotional needs of the older ones?

♥ Before our baby was born, I took several hours to record our family books onto a tape. The children listened to their favorite books with my voice during the early weeks of long nursing sessions. We do a lot of "divide and conquer" in this house; I'll give one child a job while the other helps me do something with the baby, or I contain the baby (in a sling or baby seat) while I chase the girls around the house.

Do you feel that it is important to have alone time with each child each day?

♥ Like most of the moms in this book, I believe that alone time is important, but extended periods of "alone time" are difficult to come by. When I run errands on the weekends, I like to take one of the girls with me for some special Mommy time. If my husband needs to run to his office, he'll try to take one of the children with him. I have about 5 minutes alone with each one everyday when I tuck them in for their nap or rest time. Usually, we read a story and sing a song. (Of course, the baby gets tucked in first for this to work!) They look forward to those times right before nap, and I try to impress on them the importance of not interrupting this special time for their siblings.

Do your children have overlapping social groups? How do you arrange for them to see friends or have friends come over?

♥ Right now, my children don't have unique friends. They play with any child, young or old, if I invite another family over for a play date. I suppose, as my children grow, this may change. I hope and pray that no matter what other friends my children make, they will always be each others' best friends.

How do the older children feel about taking on so much responsibility with managing younger siblings, and how do the younger ones feel about having to obey the older ones?

♥ I don't have any older children right now! So, I pass!

How do you respond to others who say that large families are poor stewards of the earth because of carbon footprints and garbage output?

♥ Watch *Demographic Winter* (*3) and *The Baby Wars* (*4)! These entertaining and informative documentaries give a great overview of the falsehoods about overpopulation that permeate our culture.

When You *Really* Need a Break

When do you take care of your own hygiene?

♥   On weekdays, I wake up at 6 a.m. to walk, shower, and dress by 7 a.m. During that hour, my husband is "on duty" for the children. Until I had two children, I just slept until the baby woke up, but now, it has been great for my mental health to rise before the children, get some exercise, and get in a shower before needing to give all day long. I usually take Sunday morning off from walking, but still wake at my regular time. This gives me some extra time on Sunday mornings to shave, put on make-up, do my hair, and maybe even trim or paint my nails. In a small way, I feel that looking my best for church is like preparing to be the bride of Christ.

What types of "beauty routines" did you do before you had children that you can't continue now? How do you handle this?

♥   I used to pluck my eyebrows every morning. Looking back, this was probably quite excessive. I'm also toying with the idea of only washing my hair once a week, but still showering every morning. I also used to fix my hair every day, either by using the blow-dryer, or braiding it. Now, I just usually put it in a pony-tail. These small changes have totally been worth it. I was too vain before, anyway!

Do you have time to exercise (besides running after the children)?

♥   I usually go for a walk first thing in the morning. Once or twice a week, my husband and I visit the YMCA, often letting the children play in the babysitting room. This workout is usually more intense than just walking, and it gives us some quite time to talk without the children interrupting.

How close are your closest friends? How often do you hear from them or get together?

♥ I have been so blessed; sometimes, I become exhausted just trying to keep in contact with everyone! I have many casual acquaintances from church and various Bible studies or play-groups. I live in a really a great community for young moms who want to be involved.

♥ I have about ½ dozen good friends that I make an effort to send cards to and call on the phone at least once a month. These are friends from growing up. I also have three really dear friends, to whom I can pour my heart out. Two live far away; the other lives just across the street. God has lavished so many blessings on me! My mom and I are also close and email and talk on the phone every week. I am blessed to spend time with her for a few days every month or so, even though she lives several hours away. Even though I have such dear friends, my husband is by far my best friend and the love of my life.

What hobbies are large-family friendly?

♥ Did I ever have hobbies? I don't really remember. It seems like it was a different life! I used to enjoy music lessons; I still love music, but only practice piano about 5 minutes a day after I play our morning hymn. I've always loved reading, but realize that I get too involved in the stories or information to stop without anger when the children need some help or attention. So I don't read much when they are awake. I go in spurts with scrapbooking; when I get out my supplies, I work for several nights in a row after the children are asleep. Since having a child with food allergies, I'm developing the new hobby of nutrition and healthy cooking. The children are pretty involved with this! I would like to continue growth in my hobbies to model the love of learning for my children; but I certainly would never want them to get the impression that these hobbies are more important than they are or they are a bother for interrupting me.

♥ There are so many things I wish I could volunteer for, given enough time and energy. Formally, I don't do much organized volunteer work, except for leading our local La Leche League monthly meetings. However, we try to bring meals to families who are in need, make cards for people who are in the hospital, and attend fund-raising benefit types of events.

How do vacations work for your large family?

♥ Our vacations have been primarily visiting family. They've always been very good at taking care of our tummies. We've also spent 2 or 3 nights away to visit historical sites. Camping has always been family friendly, as long as the weather and bathrooms are decent!

♥ For vacation with just our immediate family, I try to pack most of our food, expecting to eat "out" only one meal a day. I'll often freeze pre-cooked meals and keep them in our cooler. We usually try to simplify meals, rather than have several courses. I have been trying to keep our choices healthful, though, as I've noticed our family has a propensity to become ill during travel with all of the disruptions.

Learning Time

What special considerations are there for parents of big families when choosing an education for their children? How did you make that decision?

♥ Families with a wide age-range of children would be enrolled in several different schools at any given time. Preschool, kindergarten, grade school, middle school, high school, college ... I don't know how the mother of a large family could keep her sanity running them around to any school—public or private! Homeschooling seems like an obvious choice, to me, for large families!

♥ Homeschooling would also seem the default education choice for families who value a stay-at-home mom. Unless a definite choice is made that a school would be of benefit to a specific child, the children would continue to remain at home as they have been. I'm not necessarily opposed to school as a valid choice, but it seems to me that society has reversed norms, with school having displaced the home as the default. This seems backward.

For those of you who homeschool, how do you balance between your own household activities (such as cooking meals) and teaching your children?

♥ At one point in time, I played with the idea of having my children wear "school uniforms" when we do "school." But now I realize that we'll be doing "school" all day long! We don't spend many hours a day on schoolwork, since I work with one daughter on preschool skills, and the other on kindergarten skills. We try to get our morning housework done before doing our calendar, preschool/kindergarten activities, and read-aloud. Mid-morning, I usually play pretend with them for 20 minutes or so, and then do housework, like food-prep or organization, until lunch at 11 a.m. Occasionally, in the late-afternoon, my husband will give the girls a reading or history lesson, but this is not scheduled at all. As the girls get into higher level schooling lessons, we'll buckle down to a more predictable schedule, but this works for us now. In the evenings, we reserve the time from 5 to 6 p.m. for activities.

Do homeschoolers differentiate between normal family activities and "school" time? If so, how?

♥ At this point in time, I don't really need to. My children are still quite small and lessons and life fit together very well.

Do you have schedules for things like computer time or piano practice?

♥ None of my children have piano lessons or play the computer yet. I was hoping to get some good advice for the future in this area. We do have a specific movie time, though: after rest-time, before snack. They watch together for ½ hour. This works pretty well, and because of the predictability, they usually don't ask to watch a movie at any other time of the day. We don't have television reception, so I am able to preview all of their shows on VHS and DVD.

Do your children have activities such as a sports or music lessons? With so many different schedules, how do you get them to and from activities. Are you ever able to participate?

♥ A lot of our activities revolve around our involvement in the YMCA, which offers concurrent sessions for different age groups/skill levels. My husband or I often will take one child alone to some other activity and then we get some one-on-one (or one-on-two) bonding time. Now that my oldest is starting to be involved in some activities like Sunday School and Vacation Bible School, I have noticed that I am not as involved as I would be if I didn't have other children to tend to. But it doesn't really bother me. I think it's good for her to get used to having to obey other authority figures.

What general advice do you have for homeschooling moms with many children?

♥ I don't know yet, but I imagine that I will never regret the time I'm spending with my children, shaping their lives, and helping them grow in their faith. Regardless of the hard times involved in helping my children become educated persons, I cannot entrust this responsibility to anyone else.

The "Wife" Part of Being a Mother

Children (and a gushing wife!) are so excited to see Dad when he comes home from work! What are your tips for not overwhelming him?

♥ We all expect that Daddy will need to change clothes every day when he comes home, so we happily say hello, and expect that he will need to disappear for a few minutes once he arrives. I think this gives him a little quiet time before the kids jump him! He also generally walks to and from work, so he has a chance to unwind before he gets here.

Do you have alone time with your husband every day without the children interrupting?

♥ We usually have about 15 minutes in the morning, and an hour or so in the evening on the good days! Since I'm not a morning person, and he is, mornings are not the best time to communicate anything important! If neither of us has an activity in the evening (Bible Study, Choir, La Leche League, etc), then we have from about 7–9 p.m. together. Each time we've added a child, their bedtime has moved earlier and earlier! We're loving the 7 o'clock bedtime for them!

How often do you go on dates?

♥ As of tonight, we're starting to have a date on the 1st, 3rd, and 5th Thursdays of the month (we have activities on the 2nd and 4th). I hope this will work well, since we can't really afford to pay a babysitter every week, but a date once a month seems too infrequent. To save money, we'll have dinner with our children at home on most date nights, but go out to share a special dessert which we can savor.

Do you ever get away for a few days? How do you arrange for this?

♥ We've gone away for a weekend twice in our marriage. Once, I was still breastfeeding and had to pump. It didn't seem worth taking the trip for all the trouble of pumping! The other time, after the baby had weaned, was very nice. Two nights away was long enough to get refreshed, but not too long that the children were miserable without us. My parents were wonderful in keeping the children those two times! However, as our olive shoots increase, and my parents age, I don't think this arrangement will be feasible. Once, several winters ago, we invited a young married couple (without children) to come with us to a cabin in the woods. We paid for the lodging and they watched our children for a few hours every day so my husband and I could snow-shoe and ski. This arrangement worked out really well and I'd like to do it again!

How does your big family cope with changes when your husband is not able to participate in family life as normal ?

♥   I am poor at this. My husband is so wonderful and does *so* much for our family that it is impossible for me to pick up the pieces when he is gone. I have a lot more housework when he is gone, though, so at least I stay busy enough! I often have the children sleep in my room with me when my husband travels. I tend to catch up with friends on the phone when he is gone in the evenings, so when he is home, I can spend that time with him.

At the end of the day, how do you avoid exhaustion? Do you ever feel "touched out" from meeting the needs of the children, when your husband needs you as well?

♥   Obviously, I do feel this way sometimes, or I wouldn't have asked! Since the two of us love to talk, it's nice to spend the evening just sitting on the couch after an exhausting day. I'm always quite eager for adult conversation! As for feeling "touched out," of course, neither of us is perfect, but we both try to be understanding of one another's needs and respond accordingly.

Looking back on the earlier part of your marriage and child-rearing, are there changes you could have made then that would have made now easier?

♥   I wish I would have chosen a wedding ring setting that doesn't occasionally scratch my children! I wish I would have had brothers and sisters to watch raising their children to learn from!

Spiritual Wisdom

When do you find time to have family or personal devotions?

♥   We've been trying to spread out devotions throughout the day. My husband reads from the Bible at breakfast. We're eager to try out some new "visual aids" borrowed from friends—large posters with

Bible scenes painted on them for nearly every Bible history lesson. We generally sing a hymn after breakfast. During lunch, I read the children *Little Visits with God* (*6) which has Scripture, a story, questions, and a prayer. After dinner, Ryan teaches from Luther's Small Catechism, and we practice memory work with the children. We try to remember to pray extemporaneously and mention prayer requests before we leave the dinner table. Hopefully, it will become more and more of a habit. We sing a hymn and say a prayer with the children as we tuck them into bed.

What types of devotions appeal your family which spans several age and interest levels?

♥ We use several different books. Our children are all still quite young, though, so as they grow, that age range will increase. We might try to tailor different times of days to various levels of spiritual understanding: Bible reading for Middles, lunch devotion for Littles, and Doctrine at Dinner for Bigs? We'll see. I just don't want to leave anyone out. As soon as the children learn to read, we intend for them to be reading Scripture on their own every day.

Do all of the children participate in these devotions? Do you allow the younger ones to eat or play during devotions?

♥ It seems all of our children still eat (or nurse!) during devotions. It keeps their mouths busy, so they don't talk the entire time. If the baby is finished eating, he usually plays on the floor. He's still within hearing range, though, so the Word can work.

How do you handle getting through church services or Bible study with many little ones?

♥ Whew! This makes me work up a sweat! I tease that anyone can observe the state of the children's hair at the end of church to know how the behavior went! It's not a pretty sight when we have to wrestle with them through the service! When we had only one child, she had church related books and toys for in church, and only in church. This tended to work out just fine. But, adding a second child to the pew chaos caused a lot of fighting over toys during church. Eventually, they each had a picture Bible book to look at in church and a beaded bracelet to fidget with. But when one of the bracelets snapped, sending beads all over the church floor, and pages were torn out of the Bible books, we quickly outlawed any kind of entertainment during church. Even pencils. Adding child 3 to this arrangement has worked out just fine. If I make sure Baby is well fed before the service, Daddy holds him the whole time, and the 4- and 2-year-olds flank me. They sit when I sit and stand when I stand, though often quite reluctantly. They may sit in the manner they chose, so long as their shoes are not on the pew. I have to frequently remind them of this during the service by pushing their feet off of the pew, but it's a lot better than wrestling toys away from them! I try to coach them to participate as much as possible with the liturgy and show my oldest where we are in the hymns. Often, if they have behaved well in the early part of the service, we reward them with a piece of candy during the sermon.

♥ During our church's Bible class, there is usually a treat served. Eating it entertains my toddler, and after she has eaten, she may look at Bible related books. The baby gets held, and the oldest attends Sunday School.

Do you pray with each child before bed?

♥ We try to say personal prayers after our supper devotion and say written prayers in as a group when we turn out the lights. I usually lay by the children as we sing and pray, but besides kissing them each goodnight and blessing each one individually, I don't really speak alone with them before bed. However, right before I go to bed, I enter their room and quietly pray for each.

Big families are wonderful because ...

♥ ... there's a greater chance of survival from body heat while huddling together and awaiting rescue if the mini-van crashes into a snowbank during our cold Minnesota winters.

♥ But, seriously, the children have each other, not only now for playmates, but into their adulthoods when their Dad and I will be long gone!

Appendix Three
Editor's Answers, 2016

I thought it would be interesting to compare my own answers now, with 2 additional children, to those I gave 6 years ago. After all, why not type up fun answers and put off editing this beast of a book? As of writing these answers, my children are 9, 8, 6, 3, and 1.

Domestic Tranquility

Which kitchen items help you feed your large families efficiently?

♥ Purchase of your most-needed items, whatever they may be. While this produces more dishes, it makes food prep easier because there can be more helping hands involved. For example, we often sit around the table chopping the veggies we'll need for the week. We need several cutting boards and knives for this to happen. Every hand (that can use a knife safely) helps. (We remind the children, "If you don't work, you can't eat!")

♥ I also have enough high quality baking pans that I can fill my oven to capacity. This helps me bake in bulk and freeze. We also have dozens of large plastic reusable containers on hand for freezing meals, pancakes, or broth.

♥ I use my Vitamix (*1) blender multiple times per day to make smoothies, bulletproof coffee, and batter. We have dozens of mason jars constantly rotating between the fridge, the sink, and the shelf. I make yogurt in jars in my turkey roaster. I also use my 12-quart stock pot several times a week. I use my crock pot every day. It might be nice to have another!

♥ Organize your kitchen according to how you use it. Don't be afraid to rearrange drawers and shelves to make them more useful for you. I find that having shelves, instead of cupboards, saves me dozens of arm motions a day of opening cabinet doors! Do you find yourself annoyed to always have to put away the silverware far away from the dishwasher? Make a change. Switch drawers, or maybe just decide to store them in a caddy on the table. Bless someone else with the things you don't use regularly to make space for the items you do!

Do you plan meal menus ahead of time? How do you know that you'll have enough? Do you ration?

♥ We have a diet even more "special" than before—the GAPS Diet—and several food intolerances (*2). I *have* to menu-plan, as I can't buy much of what we consume from the grocery store! Right now, I plan breakfast based on the day of the week. (Sundays we have granola and yogurt. Mondays we have smoothies. Tuesday we have eggs and sausage.) Lunch is always leftovers from supper the day before. Each night of the week for dinner is based on a different meat, and two vegetable side dishes. (Monday is fish. Tuesday is chicken. Wednesday is pork. Thursday is turkey. Friday is beef.) We have dessert about 2 or 3 nights a week. This might seem repetitive, but it makes planning and obtaining food a cinch. I can stock up and buy 4 whole chickens from the farmer for the month. I make sure to buy 12 lbs. of ground turkey a month, 2 for each Thursday dinner, and 1 for each Tuesday breakfast. It seems to work out really well, unless someone is going through a growth-spurt, or Daddy is doing a lot of extra thinking. (He claims that the brain uses 40% of his calories!)

♥ I don't always know that there will be enough. Lunch is especially tricky if we run low on food from supper the evening before! I try not to be too controlling about second-helpings, because God always provides, often in the form of something leftover in the freezer that I had forgotten about! Or, I can break out a can of olives, or add a smoothie to the meal if I need to. (We always have fresh milk and eggs on hand.) As for rationing, I usually serve plates in the kitchen for the children's protein and favorite veggie. On the table, we pass around the other veggie, and they may serve themselves as much (or as little) as they prefer. The older children and my husband always go back to the kitchen for seconds. For more information about the purpose of the GAPS Diet and recipes, check out my blog (*3).

Do your children snack on what they want when they want to, or do you have specific times and foods?

♥ We have a snack every afternoon, and there are no second-helpings on it. Usually it is a half piece of fruit and a small protein, such as a few nuts, or a slice of cheese. Aside from that snack, they do not eat between meals. While I don't have the kitchen under lock and key, they are certainly not free to peruse the cupboards or fridge in search of snacks. Surprisingly, all of our metabolisms have gotten used to this, and we really don't get hungry between meals. We consume a lot of healthy fat with our meals, and this helps to keep us satiated.

How do you clean up effectively after a meal (especially if you have one or more children in high chairs or booster seats)?

♥ This is *so* much easier now that I have older children to help! Hooray! My three older children rotate monthly between three chores: washing dishes, washing the table/highchair, and sweeping the floor. They perform their assigned task after every meal each day (with Mom or Dad helping with dishes). The 3-year-old usually runs off to play while we work, often with the baby. While we still have sticky fingers on the walls occasionally, it is so much easier than it used to be. It wasn't long ago that I had 3 children with messy hands fingerprinting the walls, while I would frantically try to wipe up the spills on the table, soak the dishes until nap time, and sweep the crumbs off the floor! I think this began to get easier when I presented the children with an object lesson: Once, after supper, I put the crumbs from the floor into bowls for the children and served it at breakfast the next day, stating emphatically that I thought they were strategically saving the food on the floor for the next day. After that, they had in mind that if they didn't want to eat those crumbs, they should pick them up and put them in the garbage, or be more careful about eating over their plates in the first place. (*No! I didn't actually make them eat it! Ha!*)

♥ Another thing that has been helpful for us is to ditch the baby bibs. Really! Okay, so we still cover the babies' clothes, but with the same cloth napkins everyone else uses. Just clip behind their necks! This streamlines the clean-up process. We just throw the dirty ones in the laundry with the other napkins, or reuse if not embarrassingly soiled.

Lots of children means lots of dishes. How do they get done?

♥ Lots of children means lots of children to help with dishes! As mentioned above, one of our older children is assigned dish duty for the month. This entails washing breakfast dishes by hand, and loading the dishwasher after lunch and dinner. (We don't have enough plates or silverware to load the dishwasher after breakfast. They wouldn't all fit in there anyway!) Mom or Dad are in charge of all of the pots and pans. Usually, these get done after dinner or after the children go to bed. We use disposable bowls on Sunday mornings to help with the church rush, and occasionally if we are rushed for another reason.

At what ages are children capable of helping around the house? Do you have your children participate in these ways?

♥ I could philosophize and theorize about this one, but how about I just tell you what our kids do? Our 9-year-old balances the family budget, writes her own blog, does our meal-planning, shovels snow, mows the lawn, and picks up the younger kids from school. Just kidding! For real, she makes breakfast, cleans the downstairs bathroom, vacuums, does her own laundry, does dishes, sweeps, washes the table, changes diapers, washes windows, organizes her possessions, waters the plants, and does her personal care. Of course, she doesn't do every thing in that list every day, and when it does happen, it's usually only after prompting even though we have a routine established. Our 8-year-old can sweep, wipe the table, wash dishes, do her own laundry, pick up toys, dust, chop veggies, and collect and take out garbage. The 6-year-old can wash dishes, sweep, clean the table, use the floor mop, take out the recycling, help hang up laundry and put things in drawers, and do errands around the house for me. The 3-year-old definitely does *way* less than his older siblings did at his age, mostly because there are older siblings to do it for him! And he goes off and plays so nicely while we work! But, he can fold and put away washcloths, pick up toys, straighten the shoes (those multiply like rabbits around here!), and wipe up spills. The 1-year-old, well, she just flits from one mess to the next. There's always next year to teach her a thing or two!

♥ We have several mini chore times during the day. There is a certain list of things each should accomplish before breakfast, including personal care and piano practice for a few. Then, after breakfast, they have their dishes/sweeping/table jobs, as well as one other extra chore, such as laundry, cleaning their lockers, wiping down the spare bathroom, or dusting. Before both lunch and supper, they do a cursory toy pick-up. After lunch and supper, they also perform their dishes/sweeping/table jobs. Often on the weekend, or over a school break, we'll do some heavier cleaning as a family and we ask them to help out with that, as well.

How can you keep up with the laundry?

♥ This answer is actually about the same as 6 years ago, listed in Appendix 2! The only difference is that my daughters do their own load of laundry on Mondays.

How do you manage all of the diapers?

♥ We use prefolds and Bummis (*4) wraps when we have the time and energy to wash them. Or when we have a child who doesn't break out in a rash with them. Or when the baby isn't having urological surgery. Or when we aren't during the first 3 months post-partum. Hmm. But really, we have used them for the last 9 months pretty faithfully. (Cloth diapers are a great way to save money. Way before the fifth kid, they've paid for themselves over and over again! So, I got back on the cloth-diapering bandwagon when I needed more money in our budget to spend on food.) As for cleaning them, we have a used washer—purchased at a neighbor's garage sale for $70—that has a cycle for super-soiled loads, and we use our regular (homemade) detergent. Nothing extra or fancy. We try to remember to hang up the wraps, but sometimes forget, and they go in the dryer. It hasn't ruined them yet!

♥ We use disposable diapers if we are going out for more than a few hours. (I just hate carrying around urine-soaked cloth in the diaper bag, even in a soak-proof container.) We also use them during the night. I've found my babies are prone to rashes if they sleep in cloth.

How often do you go shopping for food? When do you buy other non-food necessities?

♥ I definitely spend less time in actual stores than I used to, but much more time pursuing food, as in driving to get milk and eggs, calling local farmers to arrange meat pick-up, and ordering what I need from the Internet. I also have to arrange my "shopping" life around the schedules of those who provide my food. I can't get milk on the weekend, but I must do the Farmer's Market on Saturdays. It gets easier the longer I do it because I can better anticipate how much food we will need and can stock up on some items. I definitely buy more of our body products online than I used to, and I also make many of those from scratch here in our home.

Who goes shopping with you? Does it work well?

♥ When I go shopping on the weekend, often I go alone. I really enjoy having a few quiet hours to think. Sometimes I get sad when I'm out shopping: sad to be happy without my children, sad that prices are so high, sad that other people look so lonely. Once in awhile, I bring a child or two along for a short trip when not much is needed. I never take all 5 children shopping unless my husband is also along. It gets too heavy for me to push the cart with all of the children in it who need to be contained.

Money Matters

What are your money saving tips for shopping?

♥ I've had a paradigm shift with this question! While it's great to comparison shop to save money on products that you would buy anyway, I would rather spend money on healthful, quality food than on healthcare to repair the damage done by a cheap diet. I've learned this the hard way. Our budget for food is much larger than I ever would have imagined, but we're eating well, and repairing our health naturally. I remind myself that wholesome food is *not* expensive, it is actually worth every penny that it costs. So much of the food found in the grocery stores these days is only cheap because of government subsidies. It is unnaturally cheap, and is often not good for the body. Good food is a gift that money *can* buy, with lots of time in the kitchen and preparation with love.

♥ Aside from buying in bulk, the only money-saving tip I can think of is that when I order online, I always wait until there's a sale and use coupon codes at check out! That, and plant a garden! Or help other people with their garden in the hopes that they will share! It's good for the body and soul.

Do you buy in bulk?

♥ I buy meat in bulk, half a pig at a time! We currently don't eat any grains or starches, so I don't need to order those in bulk. When I order from Azure Standard (*1), I try to buy enough dry goods for 2–3 months at a time on a rotating schedule. Other products, like toilet paper, diapers, and paper towels we buy in bulk and store in our mudroom. No one wants to run to the store just for that—especially not in the Minnesota winter!

How do you manage to keep your family supplied with toiletries like shampoo, toothpaste, deodorant, and toilet paper, on a budget?

I guess this doesn't present the same challenge as it used to. Perhaps I have just gotten used to the consumption of a large family, whereas before, it was shocking to me how much product we would go through? My children have actually been quite good about not damaging or losing their things, so when we do need a replacement, I try not to make a big deal about it. Maybe this will change when the children become teens?

How do you keep Christmas and birthdays special, but affordable?

♥ For birthday gifts, we usually buy the child one quality gift, rather than several small gifts. It's especially nice if it's something that can be passed down to siblings when it's outgrown. My husband takes the birthday child out to breakfast. This is a nice tradition for them, but also saves the money of taking the whole family out to eat. We also tell the child's birth story at supper and have a special prayer thanking God for his or her life. The child gets to choose what kind of dessert I will make that evening. We also try to remember to chart their height on a wall in the basement. I've heard of some parents instituting a new privilege and a new responsibility on each birthday, and I'd like to give that a try, as well.

♥ At Christmas, we aim to keep the focus on Jesus. We have done a few different things for gifts. We give the children small items in their stocking on each Sunday in Advent. Sometimes, we've opened a game to play on Christmas Eve. We've also had gifts for the whole family to open on Christmas, such as a mini basketball hoop, or a kiddie sewing machine. We try to reach out to make Christmas special for others by offering hospitality to someone who might otherwise be alone for Christmas.

How can you afford hair cuts for so many children?

♥ You'd think by now I'd have figured out how to use the electric hair buzzer (*2), but I'm still terrified every single time I turn it on! But usually, I face my fear and buzz my husband and sons every few months. For my daughters and myself, we go to an inexpensive hair-cutting place once or twice a year. We gals have just had too much drama (hormones?) with home haircuts in the past, so we save up money to get a professional's touch for our hair. I pay for it out of our entertainment budget. We homeschool, so anything out of the house is entertaining, right?!

Many moms in smaller families are religious about getting their children's photographs taken professionally. Is this something you do? Are there alternatives?

♥ A few years back, we had professional photos taken for our church directory. We did order some from the company and thought it was worth the cost. We have them hung up in our dining room. That was the only time we've done professional pictures. Now, however, they are outdated with the addition of another child! I'm not sure whether we will have them done professionally again, or just ask Dad to set up the tripod for our digital camera.

What are your ideas about whether or not children should receive allowance?

♥ I don't feel strongly one way or the other anymore, as if either way will ruin a child! I think it's more important to involve the children in conversations about pitching in for the family and family finances than it is to provide or not provide an allowance. That being said, we would like our children to learn to manage money and that is difficult if they do not have any—the default for our children! I would much rather have the kids pitching in regularly than having to come up with random jobs and pay for them when they are in need of cash, so we do provide a small allowance. Our 9-year-old receives $1 a week, and the younger ones go down by $0.25 per child. We do this on Sunday mornings before church so they can give a percent to church. They don't have many material desires, so they mostly save their money to buy gifts for each other! Now that the girls are a bit older, they also like to go to the fabric store with me every few months. A few weeks ago, my daughter asked for a pair of (unnecessary) shoes, but since she had just spent her money on Christmas gifts, she couldn't buy it. It was a lesson for her that was much bigger than whether or not we give an allowance. (She was logical enough to debate that she should use a Christmas gift card for them, though, so it was all good!)

What does your family do for cheap entertainment?

♥ Our children put on plays! They even came up with their own "club": the MacPherson Children's Play Company.

♥ We try to have a family game night every other Wednesday night. Sometimes, we've found it easier to split up the children into different games rather than all play the same one. I've also found, by trial and error, that I have more fun on game night when the baby has been put to bed.

♥ The children rack up pennies in a jar as a reward for good choices. Once that jar is full, we plan a special event, such as having a snack at the health food store or going to the carousel at our local mall.

♥ During the summer, we try to visit one local playground each week. We often take a picnic along.

Many families cite the high cost of college as a valid reason not to bring any more children into the world. Do you have a plan as far as college goes?

♥ We will *force* our children to attend the college where my husband works in order to receive discounted tuition! Actually, we don't really have strong feelings about them going to college. If it seems that college is something they will need in order to prepare for the vocation God is calling them into, it would be great if they could attend where Dad works. However, if it's not a good fit for whatever reason, hopefully they could apply for a scholarship elsewhere. But, perhaps they won't be led into a job that needs college anyway, so why worry about that now! Children are an eternal treasure; a college education is not.

Generally "Kid"ding Around

Are you able to keep your children's baby books current? Are there alternatives to the traditional baby book?

♥ I work really hard to keep the baby books up-to-date. By up-to-date, I mean the following: I occasionally get out the glue stick and paste some photos in there! The "dates" for when the baby first does something are crossed out, and replaced by a month or a season. I don't keep track of more than 4 teeth coming in, nor more than 1 coming out. On the pages about school information, I write, "Homeschooled. (As if they didn't know?) See school portfolio." I usually have weights for the baby's months, but never preferences, sleeping habits, or height. (Does anyone *actually* lay the baby down, stretch her out, and measure? Isn't it a little too much like torture?) There isn't much to write for the medical information. And when it comes to "Favorite Foods," I always write "Nursing." (I mean, it's true, right?) My son's "Baby Book" goes up to his 7th birthday, and I'm getting a little tired of continually filling it in.

♥ So, I do what I can with the baby book, but for the last two children, I've had more fun with making a "First Year" photobook (*3) for each of them online. I can do it in small increments over a month or two and never have to get out or put away my scrapbooking paraphernalia. I can easily order extra copies for grandparents. I think I will stick with this for the subsequent children and retire the "Baby Book" as a something *so* twentieth-century.

♥ We have continued with the "Baby Journal" tradition and try to write and update those in prose about our family life every few months. I've also included relevant Facebook status updates in the journals about cute or silly things the children say.

What is your method of getting toys picked up?

♥ Our older children are quite good about picking up when we ask them, which is usually before lunch and supper. I need to spend more time training the younger ones (... just as soon as I finish with this book). The Littles often pick up a toy or two, and then somehow find themselves in rooms unsupervised and magically reappear when all of the cleaning is done!

♥ I find it works infinitely better to assign individuals certain areas or tasks for picking up. It helps them to specifically look around and take charge of an area, rather than expecting others to do it. When I assign something specific, I can follow up with the individual if it doesn't meet inspection. There are fewer complaints about others not doing their fair share. Actually, favoring the assignment of specific domains per person with toy organization seems to be the same argument in favor of capitalism versus communism!

♥ As for their individual toys or items (rather than our general family toys), I have been known to "adopt" their things that I find left out. I put them into "hibernation" until a child asks if I have seen it. Then I truthfully answer, "Oh, yes. I have it right here! I figured you didn't want it anymore since you weren't taking care of it." Then I give it back. Usually things get put away for awhile after that.

How do you manage various appointments for all of your children? Who goes along with you?

♥ Ooh! Ooh! I have a good answer for this one! Don't go! Just say no! Well, not exactly. But, over the years, we've found it isn't nearly as necessary to do as many appointments as we thought when we were first starting out on our parenting journey. God has entrusted these children to our care. It is *our* responsibility as parents to direct their health and wellness. At first, we thought that meant pursuing all of the possible health-related opportunities available. But as we have aged, we have grown to understand that all of these appointments were actually a cop-out for us to follow someone else's recommendations for our children, rather than analyzing and judging for ourselves what each individual truly needs.

♥ We've been extremely blessed to have children with resilient health. Aside from a few pervasive problems (like special needs, food intolerance, and a urological difficulty), the children have not needed doctor's appointments. We monitor their heights and weights and developmental milestones regularly at home and keep a chart of progress. We've taken them in whenever we have had questions and consulted professionals when necessary, including chiropractors, fracture specialists, naturopaths, pediatric dentists, nurse practitioners, and speech pathologists. But, otherwise, "if it ain't broken, don't fix it!" Our primary care doctor supports our *laissez-faire* philosophy.

How do you outfit all of your children?

♥ Oh, clothes! Mother Eve, why did you ever eat that fruit and open the eyes of the world to nakedness?! (Yes, yes. I know there were bigger theological implications than that.) Unlike cleanup after meals, which has become easier as the children have grown, outfitting has become more difficult. I've had two girls in a row, followed by two boys, so you think it would be easy to hand things down, right? Wrong. The oldest girl is quite large for her age and the second is small for her age. Plus, they were born in different seasons, so there's no guarantee that what fits the first will fit the second at the right time! Also, as they get older, they don't grow as fast, so they can't automatically pass things down. Or they actually wear something out before they outgrow it. So we have the opposite problem of hand-me-downs in our house. The second gets new clothes more often than the oldest! I try to convince my oldest that it's okay because she got to wear all of the new baby clothes. As for the boys, they are just far enough apart in age that I can't pass directly from the oldest's closet to the youngest's. I actually have to pack things away for a year or two before they will fit. That is, if there is anything left that isn't torn or stained. Do you know how hard it is to find boys' pants at the thrift store? If you have boys, and a tight budget, I know you do! And then, there's the baby girl. As I get out the big sisters' hand-me-downs for her, they look faded and worn after being stored in a bin for 7 years. *Seven years.* There weren't even leggings or fashion books back then! I think all of these clothing paradoxes should be called Mrs. Murphy's Law: Any hand-me-downs that should fit, won't fit.

♥ Well, back to the question. What do we do about these sizing quirks? Remember, God always provides. In fact, this last fall, I'm pretty sure He teleported a size 6 boys bin into my basement that wasn't there before. People give gifts and friends share things their children have outgrown. Once in a while, I'll buy something new from the store to round out a wardrobe. But when I'm at the thrift store or a garage sale, I always look over the larger sizes to store things away for use within the next year or two. Often, I find that it's more than enough.

When it is time to leave the house, how do you make sure all of the children are clean?

♥ Wow! Quite the assumption I made back then! Now, I don't look! We often go places and upon arrival, I notice peanut butter on the toddler's face, or a booger in the baby's hair. Oh well. We keep it real. We have been blessed with the gift of making other parents feel proud of themselves when they compare their clean children to ours. (For your information, spell check does not recognize the word "booger.")

How do you get into and out of the house efficiently—hats, coats, shoes, bags?

♥ I try to plan ahead and get the diaper bag and my purse in the car ahead of time, so when I'm lugging the baby's carseat carrier and my coffee mug, I can somehow manage to help the toddler with his boots, zipping his coat in just the right way so he wouldn't have a melt-down, while reminding the oldest to bring along her bag, and the other daughter to go back and brush her hair and the son to quit picking on his brother and put his socks on already, and where are my keys, and didn't you already go to the bathroom, and quick grab me a few diapers from the bedroom because I can't remember if there any in the diaper bag in the car, and drat: I just noticed the spit-up on my top and I never got around to brushing my teeth, and we're already 10 minutes late, and don't forget to grab the cell phone from the charger station in case I need to call 911 because I trip on the step on the way to the garage trying not to spill my hot coffee on the baby. Whew.

♥ But, like I was trying to say earlier: They don't all have to get ready at once. Send them to get ready a few at a time and then train them to get into the car and buckle up without fighting, and wait for you indefinitely. Perfect. Doesn't it come naturally to everyone?

How is your bathroom, and bathroom time, organized?

♥ I'm so petty and spoiled. About once a week, I have to wait to use the toilet (I almost said, "go potty") when I first wake up. As I stand and wait, in my head, I grumble and think bad words and weep that I was ever born to such an existence as this. Then, I have a cup of coffee, and things don't look so bad.

♥ But seriously, our two oldest have a bedroom and a bathroom downstairs! That leaves only 5 of us to use the main bathroom. Well, 4 really, since one is still in diapers. But she does like to crawl in and play with the toilet paper and potty water.

♥ I don't really shower much anymore. So that helps. And the kids only bathe once a week. They each have their own towel, and are strictly forbidden to use any other towel they may find in the house. And I actually can't remember the last time I washed those towels. So maybe I'll take a break from typing and get that done. ...

What is the rooming situation with all of your children? Does it work well?

♥ We still have two bedrooms upstairs! One is still for my husband and me (and the baby when she was night-nursing), and one for the boys. And sometimes the baby. You see, the baby doesn't really like to go to bed. And sometimes, when she's protesting, we feel bad for the boys, so we send her to The Dungeon. (It's actually a really nice guest bedroom in the basement with a spare playpen.) But she does have a playpen upstairs in the boys' room and naps there. The older girls sleep in their own bedroom in the basement. Eventually, we plan to move the boys to the guest room downstairs. But since we don't need to yet, we enjoy using that spare room for hobbies, such as sewing, puzzles, and baby-training.

How do you find time to care for the physical needs of the baby (like feeding, bathing, and potty-training) while meeting the emotional needs of the older ones?

♥ It's not really the youngest one who needs this. It's the second youngest. The baby's life depends on attention from Mom, so the toddler's desires can be put off until need for attention explodes. This is really hard, because I always feel most bonded to my nurslings. Once they wean, I detach a bit and lose one important mothering tool. It's always a several-year adjustment for me!

♥ Right now, I try to give my 3-year-old special attention in several ways. I try to read him a story each morning after I have nursed the baby, while my oldest is making breakfast. I also have "preschool" with him for a few minutes after lunch, when we sing a song together, do a short activity, and read a story. I also often lay down by him at bedtime and rub his back. Still, it seems his "love tank" has a hole in it, and he just needs more and more of me!

♥ I've learned the hard way that I cannot try to multi-task while nursing. There's too much wiggling and movement when a toddler or older child sidle up next to us. I find that this physically *stretches* me too far, shall we say? I get really crabby really quickly when I am being sucked on by a small person and can't be in just the right position.

♥ As for the older kids, they're often "on their own." If we're not doing school, they're happy to have free time. They know where they can find me if they need me, and they know I have lots of work for them to help with if they are bored or whiny.

Do you feel that it is important to have alone time with each child each day?

♥ I feel guilty about this a lot, and I'm not sure if it's a legitimate concern, or a trap of the Devil to make me feel inadequate. Honestly, I don't have daily, or even weekly, alone time with each individual child. But, I do have moments each day to connect with them. I'm working hard to "be present" in each moment as my son tells me about his Lego project or my daughter describes her walk home from choir. I try to mean each kiss and hug instead of doing them automatically. We're surrounded by the whole family most of the day, and I'd like to think that that increases our total love for one another, rather than decreases what they perceive my love to be simply because we are not alone together.

Do your children have overlapping social groups? How do you arrange for them to see friends or have friends come over?

♥ We have been blessed with some wonderful friends from our church who are in the same life stage. Our children really socialize with entire families, rather than individuals. We have had play-dates with other families, but not really with individual children from those families. We'll have to see how this changes over the next few years. I'm hoping our children choose friends who can walk or bike over to our house so I don't have to be a taxi! I also would like to supervise them here, rather than have them at a friend's house, unless the parents are individuals that I really trust.

How do the older children feel about taking on so much responsibility with managing younger siblings, and how do the younger ones feel about having to obey the older ones?

♥ So far, the older children seem hungry for the responsibility, especially when it comes to the baby sister! Okay, except for changing poopy diapers. They aren't thrilled about that. But on most days, the instant they finish their schoolwork, they run to me and say, "Mom, can I watch the baby?" They also enjoy planning games for their little brothers to play, such as school or pretend. My 3-year-old especially likes to hang out with my 9-year-old. They have a special bond. Sometimes, he even seeks her out before me. (I try not to let that hurt my pride.) Thank God for big siblings! That being said, when it comes to obedience, the Littles sure don't like the authority of the Bigs. We're still working on listening skills, especially when the older children sometimes take on authority I haven't delegated to them!

How do you respond to others who say that large families are poor stewards of the earth because of carbon footprints and garbage output?

♥ I think that, in general, children in larger families are not as materialistic. They have to be resourceful because the family's budget just does not stretch as far. Societies only thrive when the population is growing; the hope for a better stewardship of the earth will only come from the next generation. And aside from all of that philosophy, my family ranks among the top for energy efficiency in our neighborhood (which averages less than 2 people per home), according to a recent mailing. Not bad for a family of seven that schools at home and flushes the toilet all day long?! Boo-ya!

When You *Really* Need a Break

When do you take care of your own hygiene?

♥ Um, can I be anonymous for this one? I only shower once or twice a week. This is not as much as I would like, but I have prioritized other things, like sleep. My husband is always good about taking care of the kids and the house if I want to run to the bathroom for awhile. But, lately, baths and showers exhaust me rather than energize me. Maybe I'll get back into a daily routine? Watch for an update in the second edition!

♥ As for other types of hygiene, I realistically only pluck my brows and shave my legs once a week. Are there other kinds of hygiene? It's been so long that I forget!

What types of "beauty routines" did you do before you had children that you can't continue now? How do you handle this?

♥ *Before I had children* seems so long ago! My sleep-deprived brain is having trouble remembering that former life. I used to do many more things daily, like showering and shaving, using lotion, and conditioning my hair. I also did things weekly, like clip and paint my nails and exfoliate. I'd like to do some of those things regularly (like *monthly* or *yearly*, even!) but they are pretty random right now. I find myself clipping my nails once or twice a month when I happen to be using the bathroom and no one is pounding on the door. I might slop some polish on my toenails in the summer if I feel I might be a social outcast for not wearing any. I guess since it's hard to remember the old days, I don't grieve for them too much.

Do you have time to exercise (besides running after the children)?

♥ I used to try to get up early before the kids woke up and walk or run on the treadmill (or outside for the 2 months a year it's appropriate where I live). But, I am not a morning person. As my health went downhill last year, I found it harder and harder to get out of bed at all, much less go running first thing in the morning. For several months, I wasn't capable of walking around the block, much less doing any serious exercise. However, as I've been healing, I've tried to get back into a routine—but not as soon as I crawl out of bed! I wait until after breakfast and my husband supervises the kids' chores while I walk, do some sit-ups, or lift some (very tiny) dumbbells. Then, we do devotion before he leaves for work. This new routine is *much* better!

How close are your closest friends? How often do you hear from them or get together?

♥ I am blessed to have a few different layers of close friends. Locally, I have a few mother friends that are dear to me. We get our families together one afternoon a week to do a craft. We also see each other at church. A couple of times a year we go out for breakfast or dinner together. When we are together with our families (a combined total of 17+ children), the reality is that we don't get to talk much, but it is a blessing to have quality Christian friends for my children.

♥ I also have a handful of "old" friends with whom I keep in touch by phone calls, emails, or letters every other month or so. We see each other about once or twice a year, at church conventions or while traveling. But again, usually our whole families are together, so it's hard to have a coherent conversation. Sometimes, that's a problem on the phone, too, but I try to have phone conversations during rest time when the children are quiet. That way, we can talk about more "juicy" issues.

♥ With advancements in technology like texting and Facebook, there are a lot more venues for motherhood support than there were when I first became a mother. As long as technology use doesn't become an obsession, it's nice that mothers in isolated areas don't need to feel so alone.

♥ Back in 2010, I talked about my mom being a close friend to me. Since that time, she was diagnosed with dementia and her health and memory have deteriorated quickly. Her absence in my life, even though she's still living, leaves an unfillable hole as I long for my mom and the grandmother to my children. I cling all the more to Jesus to salve my loneliness and await the Resurrection when all will be restored. We covet your prayers for her. You can read my further reflections about dementia at my blog (*1).

What hobbies are large-family friendly?

♥ This past summer, we got a state parks pass for $25. We visited several parks in our region and would spend half a day hiking and exploring. We enjoyed this a lot. When our family was smaller, we enjoyed biking, but we haven't done that in years since all of the children are at different biking stages. It doesn't feel safe or worth all of the effort to prepare the bikes. But hiking filled the niche perfectly.

♥ A great informal hobby is to cook and bake together as a service to others. When there are deep discounts on food, we'll purchase a few things and make freezer meals to take to people in need. We can do this at our own pace in the comfort of our own home. Aside from the extra dishes, it is the ideal way to volunteer!

♥ When I'm not watching soap operas and eating chocolate bon-bons, I like to read books about marriage and parenting (*2–7). Or write books about large families. I'm still figuring out how to keep my sanity while reading aloud to all of the kids, though. Either they are too wiggly and bump my glasses, jostle each other, interrupt the story with questions and observations, or leave me bruised from accidental elbow-ings. Maybe I need carpet squares, like Kindergarten?

How do vacations work for your large family?

♥ Back when we had fewer children, it was easier to get away for the weekend. But now, it seems to take an entire weekend to pack for going away for the weekend! So, we tend to be bipolar about vacations these days. We either do a quick overnight somewhere, so we don't have to pack much. Or by-golly, if we're going to go, we're going to go for a really long time! It's been our tradition for the last few summers to plan a family vacation to someplace nearby in the Midwest for the last week of August before my husband has to begin teaching college again. Many grade schools are back in session, so the sites tend to be less crowded, and the cabins are discounted. We pack or cook most of our food ourselves. We also make use of our educator discounts—thank you, HSLDA (*8)!—when visiting museums or attractions.

Learning Time

What special considerations are there for parents of big families when choosing an education for their children? How did you make that decision?

♥ There are lots of great theological and philosophical reasons to homeschool, but when it comes to having a large family, we may as well be practical! I'm not kidding when I say that I have absolutely no idea how I would get 5 kids out the door before 8 a.m. every morning! I have no idea how we would afford a Christian day school or a private high school. We save a ton of money by not needing stylish clothes. (Or needing any clothes at all! Every day can be pajama day!) We can reuse curricula and materials over and over. In general, the children are not exposed to the same amount of materialism as those who attend school with peers. I also don't know how I'd have the time and emotional energy to navigate through counseling the children when they have difficulties at school. As the schoolmarm here, I know quite a bit more about what's going on in each of their lives than if they were in someone else's classroom all day. It's also just simpler for Dad and Mom to make the schedule for the entire family based on what works, rather than having to fit different school schedules into the family and be a slave to them.

For those of you who homeschool, how do you balance between your own household activities (such as cooking meals) and teaching your children?

♥ We have a pretty consistent schedule for "school." Sometimes I do food prep or cleaning between helping them with school. Most of the formal lessons are completed between 9:00 and 11:30 a.m., which leaves a lot of time during the rest of the day to manage the home. I find that with both school and housework, disciplining myself (or the children) to do a little bit consistently every day goes a long way in accomplishing great things.

♥ When you do have a moment to relax between school and home, enjoy some humorous insight about life, balance, and kids from one of my favorite blogs, Concordian Sisters of Perpetual Parturition (*1).

Do homeschoolers differentiate between normal family activities and "school" time? If so, how?

♥ The main way we differentiate between the two is that during school hours, the children constantly hear me say, "Shhh! This is school time." Otherwise, we do keep school hours in the morning with our main curriculum, such as math, language, history, and science. During the rest of the day, we also try to encourage learning and discovery, but it's not as if I ring a bell when school's out.

Do you have schedules for things like computer time or piano practice?

♥ We've just set up a computer in the basement with a few programs like chess and typing lessons, but we don't need a schedule for that yet. Until we teach them to use it, it's not in high demand! However, we do have two children taking piano lessons (with Mom). One is scheduled to practice before breakfast. The other practices after supper. I can see this becoming tricky as we add a few more musicians to the mix. When will Baby nap with all this racket, uh, I mean, music?!

Do your children have activities such as a sports or music lessons? With so many different schedules, how do you get them to and from activities. Are you ever able to participate?

♥ Up until the last year or so, we had mostly been planning activities around Mom's and Dad's schedules. As we've added extracurriculars for the children, the two of us parents have really had to cut back. We were burning ourselves out with activities most evenings of the week! As we add in a new activity for a child, we have started to really be cautious and figure out what we can cut to keep balance.

♥ There are many, many reasons I'd like to move out into the country, but one huge blessing of living in town is that my children can walk to their activities. Since we are only a one-car family, we are blessed that the older children can walk to our church once a week to participate in a children's choir sponsored by the Christian day school there. We've also had them walk a few blocks to the local public school to take chess lessons. This has really minimized my stress since I don't have to arrange to have the car that day in the first place, wake up children from naps, pack the car, and drive around town for activities.

♥ I have to admit, we do significantly fewer activities with the younger children than we did with the older children when they were at the younger ones' ages. But they don't seem to notice or care. Back then, I believe I was motivated not so much by a desire to give my kids an advantage, but just to find things to do to help our monotonous days pass quickly. Now, I don't seem to need anything extra to speed our days along!

♥ Another thing to keep in mind with activities and big families is to maximize extracurriculars where many different ages can participate together. The past two years, my daughters and I have enjoyed being part of American Heritage Girls (*2). It's great that we can all go together to this fun learning experience and spend time with Christian friends.

What general advice do you have for homeschooling moms with many children?

♥ Find what works for you. Just because my degree is in Elementary Education doesn't mean I have to make elaborate lesson plans or create fancy bulletin boards based on Bloom's taxonomy. Homeschooling can be a heavy burden, but it doesn't have to be. Read books or talk to others to find your philosophy and go with it. I prefer very little preparation, so I lean toward scripted curricula, like Saxon Math (*3), First Language Lessons (*4) and Teach Your Child to Read (*5). If you can be faithful to do a little each day, it will all get done eventually.

♥ I also find it helpful not to compare what we are doing with other families. It's really great to chat with other parents about what curricula they use, but don't always be tempted to try something else, unless what you are doing really isn't working. Have patience with yourself and your children. And also let your children be led by their interests.

♥ On a more philosophical note, I try to remind myself on those hard days that I'm not homeschooling so my kids can be extra smart, or even just to shield them from the falsehoods that may be taught in schools. I'm keeping them home so we can concentrate first and foremost on the Lord, and secondly to help them hone the skills they will need for whatever vocations God may call them to. This definitely includes the thought that the world will become more and more evil as we approach the end times. What can the Lord do through me now to build them up in God's Word, help them memorize Scripture and hymns, and prepare them to stand firm in the faith no matter what the future holds? That's really what our decision to homeschool is all about.

The "Wife" Part of Being a Mother

Children (and a gushing wife!) are so excited to see Dad when he comes home from work! What are your tips for not overwhelming him?

♥ My husband has learned to deal with this pretty well by giving us all a short greeting and retreating to our bedroom to change into play clothes. Often, if supper is not in imminent danger of being burned, I will hasten to the bedroom with him and talk for a few minutes until the wee ones come and bang on the door.

Do you have alone time with your husband every day without the children interrupting?

♥ The only time this is guaranteed is when they are all sleeping. We may have a few minutes before they wake up or after he comes home from work, but it's not much. We've learned, after many failures, that we just cannot talk about serious matters while they are awake. This was a long realization in coming. When we only had one small child, we could talk about whatever we wanted at supper. That started to get harder with a talkative toddler and a grunting baby. When the third child was old enough to add his voice to the mix, we were totally outnumbered and gave up on having much adult vocal time during the kids' waking hours.

How often do you go on dates?

♥ Our current pattern is to go every other Wednesday night, alternating with game night in non-Advent or Lenten seasons. How's that for a pattern-oriented answer?! A couple of times a year, we do a day trip together—mostly when we need to buy furniture or remodeling supplies, because we can't fit both those and the children in our vehicle at the same time.

Do you ever get away for a few days? How do you arrange for this?

♥ We've done this every year or two (depending on pregnancy and nursing), but we couldn't do it without careful budgeting. You see, in order to get away, we have to hire sitters for as long as we're gone. We don't have any family that is able to help us with this anymore. Each time we've done it, we've been able to hire a young married, childless couple from the local Lutheran college or seminary to tag-team. Imagine them coming to live in our house with our kids for the weekend! It sure is a quick initiation into the reality of parenthood!

How does your big family cope with changes when your husband is not able to participate in family life as normal ?

♥ For context, back when I wrote this question, my husband was suffering from a herniated disc. He was in constant pain. I was left to tend to my 4-month-old and 24-month-old, 24 hours a day. Thank God for modern surgery to repair him! It was an extremely trying time in our marriage.

♥ With that in mind, when my husband is gone a few days to travel for work, you'd think things wouldn't be so bad! We try to make due by talking on the phone in the evenings from far away. When Daddy's traveling, we're thrilled for the phone to ring so he can update us about his location and any excitement that is happening. While he's gone, I also often stay up late, read a good book, and pine for him. I try to plan extra in-house activities (crafts, movies, organization) for the rest of us to do since Dad isn't around in the evenings to entertain the kids.

At the end of the day, how do you avoid exhaustion? Do you ever feel "touched out" from meeting the needs of the children, when your husband needs you as well?

♥ I just asked my husband if he thinks I feel this way. He answered, "Sometimes, but then I let you go be by yourself and read a book for awhile. And then, you're nicer."

♥ I don't feel that this is much of an issue anymore. Maybe it's where I am with nursing a toddler, which (in some cases) is much less often than a younger baby. Maybe it's also that there has been a longer space between our babies as I've aged, and so I've had a few more months between each one to get "un-touched"? At the time I began editing this book, I had 3 children 3 years and younger; I've actually never had that spacing replay itself since.

Looking back on the earlier part of your marriage and child-rearing, are there changes you could have made then that would have made now easier?

♥ I should have asked these moms more questions! What philosophies led you to have a big family? What are your thoughts on discipline and siblings fighting? How do you pay for healthcare? How do you unclog the toilets from so much ... well, you get the idea!

♥ There are three things that I wish I would have realized earlier. I am still learning and practicing every day. 1) Don't rush the kids. Give them enough time. If you don't, all sorts of vices (from you and them!) will ensue. 2) Don't have expectations. I'm not talking about following through on discipline here. I just mean, when you expect something (especially in a situation when it wasn't called for), you can be disappointed. This goes for my expectations for myself, for my husband, and for my children. I often think to myself, "Well, this isn't how I thought ____ would be." But I need to remind myself that I don't need to be in control of everything, and I will miss out on God's wonderful creativity unfolding in every situation if I demand my own expectations. 3) Give thanks in all circumstances, for this is the will of God for you. Don't just give thanks about something *else,* but find something, here and now in this situation, that God is doing to bless you (*1).

Spiritual Wisdom

When do you find time to have family or personal devotions?

♥ We've worked devotions into our regular daily routine in several different ways. My husband reads a chapter of the Bible at breakfast every morning and we discuss it. After breakfast clean-up, we do a short devotion as a family in the living room, singing a hymn and having a prayer. I purchased a listening device (*1) that has the whole Bible recorded onto it and I listen to it when I go for a walk. The children read their Bible story books (*2–7) in their beds in the evening before going to sleep. The pinnacle of our devotion life is on Sunday afternoons, where we review the Gospel lesson from church, remind ourselves of virtue traits and family rules, and discuss our upcoming week (*8).

What types of devotions appeal your family which spans several age and interest levels?

♥ I agree with the moms in the body of the book that the Bible does appeal to all ages. That wasn't on my mind a decade ago. I thought we would need to tailor everything to be in each child's zone of proximal development! Now, though, it is clear to me that the Holy Spirit can work on each of our hearts wherever we are because He promises that there is power in His Word. Find more Bible-based resources for your family at The Hausvater Project (*9).

Do all of the children participate in these devotions? Do you allow the younger ones to eat or play during devotions?

♥ During the breakfast Bible reading, often some of the children are still eating, or the baby is finished and playing on the floor. When we do our morning devotion after chores, everyone does sit in the living room and participate. The baby and the toddler are often a challenge, though. I've really had a tough time training my babies not to squirm on my lap. For the most part, I haven't had really cuddly babies; they want to get down and explore, or if I insist on holding them, they insist on nursing! But, even the toddler can answer some of the familiar responses from the liturgy, fold his hands while we pray, and stand while we recite the creed. We also reward them for good behavior and participation after devotion. They can earn up to two tokens each morning. When the tokens are all used up, we celebrate with both a special family activity and a gift to a local charity, and start the tokens over again.

♥ Another great way to encourage little ones to worship is through music (*10, 11). We have a few CDs that sing words straight from Scripture, and when we put those on during the day, it is very uplifting. Everyone likes to join in!

How do you handle getting through church services or Bible study with many little ones?

♥ I give them all to my husband and go sit alone in the nursery! Just kidding! Sometimes that sounds like a nice idea, though! Several years back, we put a ban on toys and food in church. That, and moving to the front of the sanctuary, has really helped us. Then, instead of trying to distract a noisy child, I just quietly narrate what is going on, based on the age of the child. For my 13-month-old, I will whisper, "Where is the pastor?" And she can actually see him and point. My 3-year-old loves to watch communion, and my 6-year-old usually follows along with the entire service and hymns in the hymnal. It's not foolproof, and we still usually have to take out at least the baby during church for her loud noises, but we never let anyone play if they are taken out of church. I think having a daily devotion at home helps the children know what behavior is expected of them in church, and also helps to familiarize them with the liturgy. I am often thankful that my parents and teachers had me memorize so many hymns as a child, so I can still sing along with the congregation when I'm in the narthex with the baby. I hope to pass that tradition down to the next generation. I also have to remind myself about keeping my expectations lower. I do not permit distracting or disrespectful actions from the older children. However, sometimes I'm too nit-picky about things that don't matter ("Stop twisting that ribbon! Leave your shoes on!") that I end up becoming a "behavior judge" instead of gaining the benefit of listening to the pastor myself. It is a blessing, too, to have so many older folks at church encourage us and notice when the children are well-behaved and compliment them, or alternatively, tell us things really weren't *so* bad when there's a rough day!

Do you pray with each child before bed?

♥ We eat supper together as a family pretty late, and by the time we finish, it is nearly bedtime for the younger children. So before we excuse them to brush teeth and get ready for bed, we say prayers together as a family. We go around the table and each thank God for something about our day and ask God's blessings on someone else. Then the younger children are prepared for bed by Daddy and I help the older children clean up the kitchen. Usually the Littles are ready for bed just about the time I am finished with dishes. Daddy and I sing a hymn with the Littles, say another prayer and turn off the lights. The last interaction we have with them before they sleep is making the sign of the cross on their foreheads (to remind them of their baptism) and saying the words, "May the Lord bless you and keep you."

♥ The older children stay up a little later and do some school work or read aloud with me. When it's their bedtime, I send them downstairs to their rooms with a hug, a kiss, and the same blessing mentioned above. I don't tuck them into their beds, but Daddy does go down a few minutes later and settles them in, turns off their lights, and does the blessing.

♥ This routine is very sacred to us. No matter how poorly the day has gone with fighting, anger, or sickness, they lie down and sleep in peace because we have all received forgiveness in Christ and can rest safely in His will.

Appendix Four

Personality Quiz

Do you remember those quizzes you used to take in those teen magazines? (Or was that just me?) This is one of those, but a little more mature. It's fun to think about the different ways God blesses mothers with personality styles and strengths. With the many different answers to the questions in the body of this book, you may wonder which moms are similar to you. Answer the following questions and find your matches below! You might just find a few "kindred spirits"!

1. I like my menu plans to be ...

    A. ... flexible.   B. ... specific.

2. When it comes to planning, I prefer to be ...

    A. ... spontaneous.   B. ... prepared.

3. I feel loved when I receive ...

    A. ... physical touch or gifts.   B. ... quality time.

4. I tend to describe myself as ...

    A. ... introverted.   B. ... very social.

5. When I need to talk, I turn to my ...

    A. ... close girlfriends.   B. ... husband.

6. For educating our children, we have chosen ...

    A. ... homeschooling.   B. ... private or public school.

7. When it comes to my mind, I am ...

    A. ... a philosopher.   B. ... a pragmatist.

8. My parenting style takes after ...

    A. ... Dr. Dobson.   B. ... Dr. Sears.

9. When it comes to health choices, I trust

    A. ... Western medicine.   B. ... holistic alternatives.

10.   Regarding my appearance, I prefer to ...

    A. ... look put-together.   B. ... be laid-back.

The following answers pair mothers from the body of the book with the personalities listed above.

1.   If you prefer A, you may be similar to Ann, Betsy, Sharon, Sheri, Lyn, and Laurie.

    If you prefer B, you may be similar to Karina, Dana, and Tina.

2.   If you prefer A, you may be similar to Kate, Karol, and Sharon.

    If you prefer B, you may be similar to Janet, Christy, Tina, and Lissa.

3.   If you prefer A, you may be similar to Sarah and Dana.

    If you prefer B, you may be similar to Lissa, Amy, and Christy.

4.   If you prefer A, you may be similar to Betsy and Karina.

    If you prefer B, you may be similar to Kate, Tina, Reba, and Ann.

5.   If you prefer A, you may be similar to Laurie, Reba, and Dana.

    If you prefer B, you may be similar to Amy, Sarah, and Betsy.

6.   If you prefer A, you may be similar to Sheri, Lissa, Janet, Lyn, Harriet, and Diana.

    If you prefer B, you may be similar to Kate, Betsy, Tina, and Shannon.

7.   If you prefer A, you may be similar to Karol, Sarah, and Dana.

    If you prefer B, you may be similar to Betty, Sheri, and Lissa.

8.   If you prefer A, you may be similar to Mery, Betsy, and Kate.

    If you prefer B, you may be similar to Karol, Tina, Laurie, and Sarah.

9.   If you prefer A, you may be similar to Laurie and Shannon.

    If you prefer B, you may be similar to Kate, Ann, Harriet, Karol, Karina, and Amy.

10.   If you prefer A, you may be similar to Sheri and Kate.

    If you prefer B, you may be similar to Ann and Christy.

Appendix Five
Discussion Questions

Grab your journal or some friends and reflect on the following questions as you read through the book!

Chapter 1: Domestic Tranquility

1. What is your favorite tip from this chapter?

2. Is there a certain item you think would be helpful for you to add to your home in order to serve your family better? Is there an item you don't need in your home that you could use to bless another family?

3. What is your own comfort level with domestic organization? Are you satisfied with your routines and habits?

4. How does your attitude about your own chores affect those in the home whom you serve?

Scriptures for Reflection:
1 Timothy 5:10; 1 Corinthians 14:40; Matthew 16:24–25; Matthew 6:31–34; Psalm 128

Chapter 2: Money Matters

1. What are your favorite money-saving tips? Is there a specific idea from the chapter that you would like to implement?

2. Why is it important to you to be a good steward of God's blessings?

3. Brainstorm some cheap or free wholesome entertainment ideas.

4.   As the children grow older, they sometimes embark on more expensive adventures. How do you balance preparing for those costs and yet trusting fully in God to provide?

Scriptures for Reflection:
     Matthew 6:19–21; Luke 16:10–13; Luke 6:38

Chapter 3: Generally "Kid"ding Around

1.   Do you have any guilt about treating your children differently or showing favoritism? What do you do to deal with it?

2.   Our children look to us for so many necessities. Discuss how, ultimately, it isn't Mom who provides these things, but the Father in Heaven.

3.   When the burden of caring for our children is heavy, Jesus invites us to take up His light yoke. What are some concrete ways we can turn our worries over to God?

4.   What are some ways your family can be better caretakers for the earth and God's creation?

Scriptures for Reflection:
     Matthew 6:25–30; Philippians 4:6; 1 Peter 5:6–7; Psalm 37:25; Galatians 6:9–10; Matthew 10:42

Chapter 4: When You *Really* Need a Break

1.   Where does taking care of yourself rank on your to-do list?

2.   Discuss the Bible's analogy of the body being the temple of the Holy Spirit. How does this apply to your exercise program?

3.   Reflect on society's emphasis that women deserve pampering time. How does this fit with Christ's directive to take up our cross and follow Him? Where is the balance?

4.   How are you a Christian friend to others? How could others be a good friend to you?

Scriptures for Reflection:
   Isaiah 40:11; Isaiah 40:29–31; 1 Corinthians 6:19–20; James 1:12

Chapter 5: Learning Time

1. What is your family's educational philosophy? Which mothers in this book seem to be on the same page as you?

2. Are you content with the school situation for your children?

3. What works well about your school and activity schedule? What needs tweaking?

4. Is this a time in your life when your family should simplify, a time to hold the course, or a time to add in more experiences?

Scriptures for Reflection:
   Job 34:2–4; 2 Timothy 3:15–16; Psalm 111:10; Deuteronomy 6:4–7; Ecclesiastics 3:1–8; James 1:5

Chapter 6: The "Wife" Part of Being a Mother

1. If you don't regularly get time alone with your husband, what changes might you make to create time for it?

2. What are your favorite date ideas? What would you like to do that you haven't?

3. Pretend that you are your husband. What is one thing in your marriage that he would like to improve?

4. Do you have any regrets from earlier in your marriage? Where do you find true comfort?

Scriptures for Reflection:
   Ephesians 5:22–24; 1 Corinthians 7:4–5; Hebrews 13:4–6; Proverbs 5:18–19; Proverbs 12:4; 1 Peter 3:1–6

Chapter 7: Spiritual Wisdom

1. In what ways are you following God's command to disciple your family?

2. How can you support your husband as he serves as your family's head of house?

3. After reading this chapter, what ideas did you gain for making church attendance go more smoothly?

4. Reflect on some of your family traditions. How can you bring God's love into them?

Scriptures for Reflection:
    1 Timothy 2:11–14; Matthew 18:5–6; Psalm 127; Proverbs 22:6

Appendix 1: Wisdom from Mature Moms

1. Which encouragement from this chapter did you find most comforting?

2. Is there anyone in your church or community you could ask to mentor you? Is there anyone you could mentor?

3. Why is your big family wonderful?

Scriptures for Reflection:
    Titus 2:3–5; Proverbs 14:1; 1 Peter 5:5; Isaiah 66:12–13; 2 Corinthians 5:17

Appendix Six

Recommended Resources

Websites are current as of January 2016. The editor has not reviewed all resources; they are given at the recommendation of the contributors. Enjoy, and use with discretion.

Please note that I am an affiliate for several different marketplaces. If you choose to buy a product listed in this book, I would appreciate it if you would use the website or link provided, as a fraction of the profit will support me and my family. For an electronic copy of this appendix, with active hyperlinks to each resource, visit:

www.intoyourhandsllc.com/training/materials/70

Chapter 1: Domestic Tranquility

1. Cindy Rushton's *Brain-in-a-Binder*:
   http://www.cindyrushton.com/MYOBIBEBOOK.html

2. Donna Young's Website:
   http://www.donnayoung.org/index.htm

3. Clean 'n' Flip Zone Cleaning for Kids:
   http://www.timestales.com/ZoneBuy.html

4. Shower Wands:
   http://amzn.to/20htJ5C

5. The Maxwells' *Managers of Their Homes*:
   http://amzn.to/1P8M2q6

6. Fly Lady:
   http://www.flylady.net

7. Toilet Sprayer Wand:
   http://amzn.to/1ZFBobT

8.   Elimination Communication Information:
     http://www.diaperfreebaby.org

9.   Melaleuca:
     https://www.melaleuca.com

10. Don Aslett's Cleaning Center:
     http://shop.cleanreport.com

Chapter 2: Money Matters

1.   Freecycle:
     https://www.freecycle.org

2.   Foaming Hand Soap Dispensers:
     http://amzn.to/1S9Z5Zk

3.   Netflix Alternatives:
     http://faithflix.net
     http://pureflix.com
     http://www.faithandfamilyfilms.net

4.   John Taylor Gatto's *Weapons of Mass Instruction*:
     http://amzn.to/1PtwusL

Chapter 3: Generally "Kid"ding Around

1.   Nancy Campbell's Above Rubies Ministry:
     http://www.aboverubies.org

2.   Shonda Parker's Website:
     http://www.naturallyhealthy.org

3.   Arm's Reach Co-Sleeper:
     http://amzn.to/1SavaQt

4.   William and Martha Sears' *The Attachment Parenting Book*:
     http://amzn.to/1Vff9s3

5. Ergo Baby Carrier:
   http://amzn.to/1SaxoPO

6. Gary Chapman's *The 5 Love Languages of Children*:
   http://amzn.to/1Saxiba

Chapter 4: When You *Really* Need a Break

1. T-Tapp:
   http://www.t-tapp.com

2. La Leche League Breastfeeding Information:
   http://www.llli.org

3. VRBO:
   https://www.vrbo.com

Chapter 5: Learning Time

1. The Robinson Self-Teaching Curriculum:
   http://www.robinsoncurriculum.com

2. My Father's World:
   http://www.mfwbooks.com

3. Sonlight:
   http://www.sonlight.com

4. Dorothy Sayer's *The Lost Tools of Learning*:
   http://amzn.to/1lTlhKh

5. Douglas Wilson's *Recovering the Lost Tools of Learning*:
   http://amzn.to/1lTkQjf

6. Susan Wise Bauer's and Jessie Wise's *The Well-Trained Mind*:
   http://amzn.to/1nPBYrR

Chapter 6: The "Wife" Part of Being a Mother

1. Emerson Eggerich's *Love and Respect*:
    http://amzn.to/1lTZZMA

2. Michael and Debi Pearl's *To Train Up a Child*:
    http://amzn.to/1Schmad

3. Clay Clarkson's *Educating the Whole-Hearted Child*:
    http://amzn.to/1lU2A9n

4. L. Elizabeth Krueger's *Raising Godly Tomatoes*:
    http://amzn.to/1ScioVd

5. Debi Pearl's *Created to Be His Helpmeet*:
    http://amzn.to/1KGdoyk

Chapter 7: Spiritual Wisdom

1. Martin Luther's *Small Catechism*:
    http://amzn.to/1PDp8Ts

2. Clay Clarkson's *Our 24 Family Ways*:
    http://amzn.to/1nRK8A1

3. Concordia Catechical Academy:
    http://lutherancatechesis.org

4. John Piper's Desiring God Ministries:
    http://www.desiringgod.org

5. Listening to Luther CD:
    http://amzn.to/1PDxJpm

Appendix 2: Editor's Answers, 2010

1. Charlie's Soap:
    http://amzn.to/1o2UmgX

2.   Swanson Vitamins:
   http://tinyurl.com/mmswvit

3.   Barry MacClaren's *Demographic Winter*:
   http://amzn.to/1QlKd5L

4.   Jim Clay's *The Baby Wars*:
   http://amzn.to/2oPJfWB

5.   Hirsch's *Core Knowledge Sequence*:
   http://amzn.to/1o2URrg

6.   Jahsmann's and Simon's *Little Visits with God*:
   http://amzn.to/1KUx2qu

Appendix 3: Editor's Answers, 2016

Domestic Tranquility

1.   Vitamix Blender:
   http://amzn.to/1PVe4aS

2.   Information on the GAPS Diet:
   http://www.gapsdiet.com or http://amzn.to/23JwHT9

3.   Marie's GAPS Blog:
   http://www.intoyourhandsllc.com/component/tags/tag/3-gaps.html

4.   Bummis Cloth Diaper Wraps:
   http://amzn.to/1nO6q5T

Money Matters

1.   Azure Standard:
   https://www.azurestandard.com

2.   Norelco Hair Trimmer:
   http://amzn.to/1PiydSG

3. Shutterfly:
    https://www.shutterfly.com

When You *Really* Need a Break

1. Marie's Blog about Dementia:
    http://www.intoyourhandsllc.com/component/tags/tag/10-dementia.html

2. Jim and Charles Fay's *Love and Logic*:
    http://amzn.to/20Q90WP

3. Faber and Mazlich's *How to Talk So Kids Will Listen*:
    http://amzn.to/20Q92Ox

4. Sarah, Stephen, and Grace Mally's *Making Brothers and Sisters Best Friends*:
    http://amzn.to/1nRVBiK

5. Voddie Baucham's *What He Must Be*:
    http://amzn.to/1nRVSlz

6. Chancey and McDonald's *Passionate Housewives Desperate for God*:
    http://amzn.to/1SXZbnd

7. Walt and Barb Larimore's *His Brain, Her Brain*:
    http://amzn.to/1SXZluM, summarized at:
    http://www.hausvater.org/book-reviews/241

8. Home School Legal Defense Association (HSLDA):
    http://www.hslda.org

Learning Time

1. Concordian Sisters Blog:
    http://concordiansisters.blogspot.com

2. American Heritage Girls:
    http://www.americanheritagegirls.org

3. *Saxon Math*:
   http://amzn.to/1SGM2ka

4. *First Language Lessons*:
   http://amzn.to/1V23tsG

5. Engelmann's *Teach Your Child to Read in 100 Easy Lessons*:
   http://amzn.to/20xGJaY

The "Wife" Part of Being a Mother

1. Ann Voskamp's *1,000 Gifts*:
   http://amzn.to/1PXUOt6

Spiritual Wisdom

1. Go Bible:
   http://amzn.to/20xBrvZ

2. Joslyn Molstad's *Jesus, Our Family Guest*:
   http://amzn.to/1KvmUty

3. *Jesus Storybook Bible*:
   http://amzn.to/20xBKH6

4. *The Story Bible*:
   http://amzn.to/20xBKH6

5. Egermeier's *Bible Story Book*:
   http://amzn.to/20xCw7a

6. *365 Bible Stories for Young Hearts*:
   http://amzn.to/20xCQms

7. According to Your Word Coloring Books:
   http://accordingtoyourword.com

8. Learn more about our Family Altar Board at our blog:
   http://www.intoyourhandsllc.com/blog/60-start-a-tradition-
   the-family-altar-board.html

9. The Hausvater Project:
    www.hausvater.org

10. Seeds Family Worship:
    http://amzn.to/1K3aSYv

11. Learn by Heart Bible Songs:
    http://amzn.to/1NUAXUf

Acknowledgements

"[I] always thank God for you and continually mention you in [my] prayers. [I] remember before our God and Father your work produced by faith, your labor prompted by love, and your endurance inspired by hope in our Lord Jesus Christ."
1 Thessalonians 1:2-3

My heartfelt thanks go out to my husband Ryan, for all of your encouragement and support; for your suggestions and ideas; for your involvement in our children's lives; and even beyond this project, for making me a mother of many. I thank God for you and for how you have been such a rich blessing in my life.

Thank you to my treasures: Grace, Rose, Price, and now, Newman and Joy, too! You have been very patient as Mommy has worked on this project to be a blessing to other mothers.

Thank you to my father and mother, for bringing me to the font of baptism and raising me in the Christian faith; for being loving grandparents to my children, and for loving and forgiving me.

Thank you sisters in Christ: Deb, Tricia, Anna, Julie, Rebecca, Andy, Stephanie, and Katie for all of your love, support, talks, and tears.

Thank you to the women at Mt. Olive's Tuesday Morning Bible Study for teaching me and passing on your own mothering wisdom.

Thanks to my friends on the Simple Trust Facebook page who have supported me in my mothering journey, and in many ways, have become what I was looking for back in 2008 when I first wrote my survey.

Thanks, also, to those busy mothers who have edited this manuscript: Elizabeth Sulzle, Christina Hagan, Rebecca Brooks, Anna Gullixson, and Kim Holtz (6 years ago).

Thank you to all the wonderful mothers who took the time to answer my many, many questions: Laura T., Karen J., Stacey C., Sheryl R., Shannon C., Anne M., Melody F., Jarnette S., Debbie B., Molly S., Danielle H., Lyn W., Heather H., Dana F., Stacy M., Karen G., Rebekah C., Sharon S., Katie H., Sherry D., Lisa M., Debbie B., Anne G., LaRena S., and Kristie H. You have been an inspiration to me and to those around you.

Thanks, above all other thanks, to God for helping me bring this project to completion! Thank you for blessing me with such a wonderful family, way beyond what I deserve. Thank you, most of all, for salvation in Jesus which covers all of my mistakes and empowers me to live the life to which you have called me with peace in my heart.

About the Author

Marie K. MacPherson is wife to Ryan, homeschooling hausmutter to their five living children, and redeemed child of God. She has a bachelor's degree in Elementary Education from Bethany Lutheran College, with Lutheran school certification and a specialty in communication arts and literature. She used to actively participate in theater, debate team, choir, and international travel, but realizes now that those were merely a foretaste of the joys of her current vocation: managing children's dramatics, arbitrating kids' arguments, singing hymns and lullabies, and sharing unbelievable mission stories. She has been an advocate for mothers, serving as a La Leche League Leader for over six years and a volunteer at a local pro-life pregnancy clinic. When she's not caring for her own children, or the mothers of other children, Marie reads extensively, researching natural health, healing diets, alternative medicine, dementia, homeschooling, theology, evangelism, marriage, and parenting. Follow her blog at:

www.intoyourhandsllc.com/blog

Ordering Information

Mothering Many: Sanity-Saving Strategies from Moms of Four or More is available for individual purchase at Amazon.com and other reputable booksellers. To inquire about bulk orders for your women's group, contact the publisher at:

www.intoyourhandsllc.com/contact

Mothering Many Facebook Group

Did you like what you just finished reading? Eager for more tips and encouragement? Have questions of your own? We'd love to "meet" you! Join the continuing conversation at:

www.facebook.com/groups/motheringmany

Coming Soon!

Lessons Learned at Home:
Families Tell Their Homeschooling Stories

Christian home educators offer a unique perspective in today's complicated world of opportunities and decisions. The families represented in this book share their experiences and answer significant questions, including:

♥ *Why* do some families educate their children primarily in the home, others utilize public or parochial schools, and still others try some of each?

♥ *How* do Progressive, Classical, Christian, and Unschooling models for education differ from each other, and is it possible to integrate these philosophies into a coherent approach?

♥ *What* distinctive emphases do Lutheran, Catholic, and Reformed home education resources offer families?

♥ *How* do home educating parents coordinate their family schedules, select curricula, and track their progress?

♥ *What* have home educators done to pass muster with state requirements, make use of taxpayer-funded services, and prepare their children for the "real world"?

♥ *How* can home educators constructively address the concerns of grandparents, pastors, neighbors or others who have doubts about children not being in school?

♥ *Where* should you turn for more information, without wasting your time in the vast sea of online resources?

Whether you currently home educate your children, would like to do so, or are afraid to try, this book provides the insights you need to make an informed judgment—and to explain your choices to those who think differently.

To volunteer to participate in our homeschool family survey, or to order this book, visit:

www.intoyourhandsllc.com/publishing/books/71a

Also Published by Into Your Hands LLC

Debating Evolution before Darwinism: An Exploration of Science and Religion in America, 1844–1859, by Ryan C. MacPherson, Ph.D.

Fifteen years before Darwin's *Origin of Species* shook the world, a debate over evolution already raged in America's classrooms, churches, and scientific institutions. Vestiges of Creation, published anonymously by the Scottish journalist Robert Chambers in 1844, boldly marshaled recent scientific discoveries into a sweeping hypothesis of naturalistic development. Crafting a narrative energetic enough for lay readers, but supported with footnotes thorough enough for scholars, Dr. MacPherson reveals unexpected interactions between religion and science during this crucial era.

"Church Control or Birth Control": Margaret Sanger's Propaganda Campaign against the Catholic Church, by Nicholas Kaminsky, M.A.

The name Margaret Sanger is nearly synonymous with birth control in the United States. A controversial character even now, she founded the predecessor to today's Planned Parenthood and dedicated her life to working tirelessly for the legalization and promotion of birth control and abortion. While scholars have directed some attention toward Sanger's provocative statements on race and ethnicity, few have documented her vehement anti-Catholicism or shown the way she cleverly used anti-Catholic propaganda to promote her birth control crusade. Kaminsky has now done so. In this book, he demonstrates the way in which Sanger exploited powerful anti-Catholic sentiment in the United States to portray her fight for birth control as a struggle for American Freedom against a moral domination by the Catholic Church.

Rediscovering the American Republic, Volume 1: 1492-1877 and *Volume 2: 1877–Present,* by Ryan C. MacPherson, Ph.D.

Each volume contains over 700 pages of time-tested teaching tools, collectively spanning ten major epochs of American history: Pre-Columbian to British North America, 1492–1763; The Creation of the American Republic, 1763–1789; The Power of Political Parties, 1789–1836; Liberty, Slavery, and American Destiny, 1836–1860; The Civil War and Reconstruction, 1860–1877; America in the Gilded Age, 1877–1901; Progressive Reform and Human Nature, 1901–1929; The Emergence of the American Superpower, 1929–1953; The Cold War and Civil Rights, 1953–1981; The Triumph and the Vulnerability of the World's Only Superpower, 1981–Present.

www.intoyourhandsllc.com/publishing/books